UNDERSTANDING

CONTEMPORARY AMERICAN LITERARY THEORY

Understanding Contemporary American Literature
Matthew J. Bruccoli, General Editor

Volumes on

Edward Albee • John Barth • Donald Barthelme • The Beats
The Black Mountain Poets • Robert Bly • Raymond Carver
Chicano Literature • Contemporary American Drama
Contemporary American Horror Fiction
Contemporary American Literary Theory
Contemporary American Science Fiction • James Dickey
E. L. Doctorow • John Gardner • George Garrett • John Hawkes
Joseph Heller • John Irving • Randall Jarrell • William Kennedy
Ursula K. Le Guin • Denise Levertov • Bernard Malamud
Carson McCullers • Arthur Miller • Toni Morrison's Fiction
Vladimir Nabokov • Joyce Carol Oates • Tim O'Brien
Flannery O'Connor • Cynthia Ozick • Walker Percy
Katherine Anne Porter • Reynolds Price • Thomas Pynchon
Theodore Roethke • Philip Roth • Mary Lee Settle
Isaac Bashevis Singer • Gary Snyder • William Stafford
Anne Tyler • Kurt Vonnegut • Tennessee Williams

UNDERSTANDING
Contemporary American Literary Theory

Michael P. Spikes

UNIVERSITY OF SOUTH CAROLINA PRESS

Published in Columbia, South Carolina, by the
University of South Carolina Press

Manufactured in the United States of America

01 00 99 98 97   5 4 3 2 1

Library of Congress Cataloging-in-Publication Data

Spikes, Michael P. (Michael Paul), 1954–
  Understanding contemporary American literary theory / Michael P.
Spikes.
     p.   cm. — (Understanding contemporary American literature)
  Includes bibliographical references and index.
  ISBN 1–57003–134–7
  1. Criticism—United States—History—20th century. 2. American
literature—20th century—History and criticism—Theory, etc.
I. Title. II. Series.
PS78.S65 1996
801'.95'09730904—dc20   96–25247

For My Mother and Father, and for Ann

CONTENTS

EDITOR'S PREFACE

The volumes of *Understanding Contemporary American Literature* have been planned as guides or companions for students as well as good nonacademic readers. The editor and publisher perceive a need for these volumes because much of the influential contemporary literature makes special demands. Uninitiated readers encounter difficulty in approaching works that depart from the traditional forms and techniques of prose and poetry. Literature relies on conventions, but the conventions keep evolving; new writers form their own conventions—which in time may become familiar. Put simply, *UCAL* provides instruction in how to read certain contemporary writers—identifying and explicating their material, themes, use of language, point of view, structures, symbolism, and responses to experience.

The word *understanding* in the titles was deliberately chosen. Many willing readers lack an adequate understanding of how contemporary literature works; that is, what the author is attempting to express and the means by which it is conveyed. Although the criticism and analysis in the series have been aimed at a level of general accessibility, these introductory volumes are meant to be applied in conjunction with the works they cover. They do not provide a substitute for the works and authors they introduce, but rather prepare the reader for more profitable literary experiences.

M. J. B.

PREFACE

This book is an introduction to the thought of six major figures working in and influencing the field of American literary theory and criticism over roughly the past twenty-five years. While their work reflects a wide range of perspectives—deconstruction, black studies, new historicism, feminism, political critique, neopragmatism—it by no means mirrors all of the most important movements during this time. Indeed, each of the areas represented by these six is itself, while bound together by certain loose principles and commitments, a largely heterogeneous mix of strategies and suppositions; no single individual, including the ones featured in this book, could adequately stand for any one of these areas as a whole. Thus, my emphasis in this study is on each theorist's unique contributions rather than on his or her place in a larger school. In fact, several of these figures could just as easily be identified with other critical movements than the ones discussed here.

It would be impossible, in the limited space that this study allows, to review every text by each of these prolific theorists. Thus, I have restricted myself to examination, sometimes partial, of major books; uncollected essays and introductions to anthologies have generally been ignored. Only selected essays from collections are analyzed, and only their key arguments are the focus. Much scholarly commentary, some positive some critical, has been written on all six theorists. I present only occasional samples of this commentary, not endeavoring to register all the praise or objections that their work has elicited. My goal here is to offer brief, basic guides to the careers, key texts, and central assumptions of six authors whose work has, in recent years, significantly shaped literary criticism and theory.

UNDERSTANDING

CONTEMPORARY AMERICAN LITERARY THEORY

CHAPTER ONE

Introduction

*A Brief History of Literary Theory
in the Twentieth Century*

How do readers decide what the words of a literary text mean? How does one distinguish a valid from an invalid interpretation? Is the text's meaning the same thing as the author's intention? What is the relationship between an author's biography and the message of his or her work? What is the relationship between a reader's biography and the way he or she interprets a text? To what extent is a text's meaning determined by the cultural and historical contexts in which it was produced and in which it is read? How do literary works connect with each other? How do they connect with works of theory and criticism, philosophy, psychology, theology, law? Is there a difference in kind between literature and these other forms of discourse, or does all language signify in essentially the same way?

These are some of the important issues which constitute the subject matter of literary theory. The focus of the theorist is *how,* rather than *what,* texts mean. Theory establishes principles enabling particular acts of practical criticism. Though clearly distinct functions, criticism and theory are intimately and implicitly connected: to have a theory of interpretation is at least to suggest, if not fully articulate, specific interpretations, while to give specific interpretations is at least to suggest, if not actually spell out, a theory of interpretation. This connection is so firm that in practice the two terms are sometimes elided, one or the other standing in for both. There are books and essays almost exclusively theoretical in their focus and others almost exclusively critical, but most frequently the two forms intermix, the theorist/critic formulating strategies of interpretation which he or she applies to specific texts and the critic/theorist providing at least some rationale for his or her interpretations. All six of the figures examined in this book fall in the theorist/critic category. Their work emphasizes theoretical constructs, but these constructs are extensively applied to the reading of particular texts, both literary and nonliterary.

In order to comprehend the full significance of these six thinkers' projects, it is helpful to place them in the context of the history of theory and criticism in this century. Entire books, some of which will be cited in the following pages, have been written on the story, or specific aspects of the story, of modern literary analysis. Necessarily, then, the observations in this short introduction will be sketchy and limited, ignoring many important thinkers and movements and only summarily and incompletely presenting others. Even such a truncated overview can, however, give a general sense of the course the field has followed in recent years and help clarify the roles the subjects of this book have played and continue to play in the extension and direction of that course.

As Vincent B. Leitch points out in *American Literary Criticism from the Thirties to the Eighties,* perhaps the finest and most complete history to date of contemporary theory in the United States, many of the leading American theorists in the early part of this century were either avowed Marxists or political leftists of various other stripes. Leitch cites John Macy's *The Spirit of American Literature* (1913), Van Wyck Brooks's *America's Coming of Age* (1915), and Vernon L. Parrington's multivolume *Main Currents in American Thought* (1927–30) as examples of sociologically oriented studies with politically liberal leanings.[1] Perhaps the two most important early marxists, according to Leitch, were V. F. Calverton and Granville Hicks. In *The Liberation of American Literature* (1932), Calverton interprets the native literary canon in terms of such standard Marxist categories as the class system, economic determinism, and social forces and contradictions. He holds that criticism should be firmly grounded in a socialist vision, always sensitive to the connections between literature and the culture at large.[2] Hicks, though in his later years a staunch anticommunist, argues in *The Great Tradition: An Interpretation of American Literature Since the Civil War* (1933) for the importance of political action and the view that the best authors are those whose work exemplifies revolutionary marxist attitudes. However, he pays closer attention to the strictly aesthetic dimension of texts than does Calverton.[3]

Though sociological and political criticism were important in the first half of the century, the most influential and significant movement of this time was one which eschewed sociology and politics altogether: the New Criticism. As David Robey observes in "Anglo-American New Criticism," this movement "almost certainly constitutes the English-speaking world's major contribution to literary theory. . . ."[4] The New Criticism was hatched in England in the 1920s in the work of I. A. Richards, T. S. Eliot, and William Empson, and it flourished in this country in the 1930s,

1940s, and beyond through the books and essays of such critics as John Crowe Ransom, Allen Tate, R. P. Blackmur, Cleanth Brooks, and W. K. Wimsatt.[5] Though in recent years the New Critical approach has come under considerable attack from various quarters and has largely been eclipsed, its legacy still lives in residual forms even in today's university classrooms and most sophisticated theoretical texts.

The New Criticism, like all critical schools, was by no means a monolith of universally agreed upon ideas. It is possible, however, to identify a core of central tenets that most, if not all, New Critics generally adhered to and promoted.

(1) The poem ("poem" for the New Critics meant any literary work of art, though most of their attention was, in fact, devoted to verse rather than prose) is understood apart from its author's biography. As W. K. Wimsatt and Monroe Beardsley argued in their seminal essay "The Intentional Fallacy" (1946), the text's meaning is objectively built into the words on the page; therefore, knowledge of the author's intention is not necessary or relevant in recovering that meaning.

(2) Since the text's meaning is wholly contained in its words, it is not necessary to study the historical or cultural context in which the text was produced. The poem is "autotelic," an isolated verbal construct whose meanings can be derived from the poem by itself, apart from its historical or cultural situation.

(3) Wimsatt and Beardsley maintained in "The Affective Fallacy" (1949) that the poem's meaning should not be confused with the reader's personal responses to it. The focus of the critic should be on recovering the publicly accessible senses objectively contained in the text, not on recording any private, idiosyn-

cratic reactions which the critic might foist upon it.

(4) Literary language differs from other forms of language. Scientific language, for instance, is denotative while poetic language is connotative. Poetry is richer and more nuanced than is the straightforward scientific tract.

(5) The New Critics saw such linguistic devices as metaphor, irony, and paradox—in which opposites are brought together in various ways to form dynamic and unified tensions—as fundamental components of poetry. The good New Critical poem is a complex network of diverse ideas and images that cohere to create an organic whole.

(6) The New Critical focus is on the linguistic devices and structures through which the poet communicates his or her meaning, but these formal elements are seen as conveying a special knowledge of the real world, namely, that life is a complex experience of reconcilable opposites.

(7) The critic is always to avoid what Brooks called "the heresy of paraphrase," the mistake of reducing the poem to or equating it with a simple, abbreviated, thematic summation. His or her job is closely to scrutinize the words on the page in order to render a description of the complexities of the text's language and thereby uncover the complex insights into experience that the poem yields.[6]

Working at approximately the same time as the New Critics was another important group, the Chicago Critics, also known as the Neo-Aristotelians. Like the New Critics, they advocated the study of literature as literature rather than literature as primarily a reflection of author biography, social backgrounds, or historical periods.[7] This school of thought, whose leaders were a collection of University of Chicago professors including Richard Mckeon, Elder Olson, and R. S. Crane, did, however, differ from the New Criticism in significant ways and, in fact, was outrightly dismissive of certain important New Critical assumptions.[8] Whereas the New Critics, for example, focussed almost exclusively on the actual analysis of specific texts, the Chicago Critics, who were certainly interested in such analyses as well, also devoted a great deal of attention to the history of theory.[9] And unlike the New Critics, the Chicago group relied heavily on a methodology derived from Aristotle. As a result of this reliance, they tended to concentrate, as the New Critics did not, on distinguishing various literary "kinds"—tragedy, comedy, epic, lyric, novel—and describing each kind's special properties. They understood the individual text in terms of the ways in which it exemplifed its kind's characteristics.[10] "One of the more controversial consequences of their [the Chicago critics'] assumption that literary meaning is to be found in the (generic) intention of the text," Brian Corman observes, "is that like Aristotle, they subordinate the function of literary language to the larger structure of the work as a whole. . . ."[11] As Leitch points out, though this group is important in the history of American theory, the Chicago critics' influence was not as pervasive and has not been as enduring as that of the New Critics.[12]

One of the most sustained and significant early challenges to the New Critical orthodoxy of isolating the individual work for analysis was Northrop Frye's *Anatomy of Criticism,* which appeared in 1957. Frye, like the New Critics and Neo-Aristotelians, believed that criticism should be about literature as a separate and distinct field of inquiry. In his "Polemical Introduction" to the

Anatomy, he denounces attempts to "attach criticism to one of a miscellany of frameworks outside it" and champions the goal of finding "a conceptual framework for criticism within literature." Writes Frye: "The axioms and postulates of criticism . . . have to grow out of the art it deals with."[13] Where Frye differs significantly from the New Critics is on the nature of these axioms and postulates. He is interested in constructing an overarching, strictly literary system in which individual texts and their component parts are not comprehended by themselves, as the New Critics would have it, but rather, somewhat like the Chicago critics postulated with the notion of literary kinds, in terms of their respective places within a larger system. For example, the hero of a narrative in Frye's theory is not to be understood merely as he or she functions in a particular, isolated story, but rather as a character type with a specific role and identity determined by the type of text in which he or she appears. Terry Eagleton explains and illustrates: "in myth [in Frye's view] the hero is superior in kind to others, in romance superior in degree, in the 'high mimetic' modes of tragedy and epic, superior in degree to others but not to his environment, in the 'low mimetic' modes of comedy and realism equal to the rest of us, and in satire and irony inferior."[14] Much like the natural scientist, Frye attempts in his *Anatomy* to classify and comprehend the objects of his field of study in terms of interrelated categories derived from that field itself.

Frye's focus on literature as system paved the way for the introduction of structuralism into American theory. Structuralism was imported from France in the mid 1960s. The first significant sign of its influence can be located in 1966 with the publication in *Yale French Studies* of a special issue devoted entirely to this subject. The movement flourished from the early 1970s into the early 1980s, its leading practitioners and expositors including Seymour Chatman, Jonathan Culler, Claudio Guillen, Gerald Prince, Robert Scholes, and Michael Riffaterre.[15] Most of structuralism's principal concepts can be traced back to Ferdinand de Saussure, a French linguist whose views are recorded in the landmark *Course in General Linguistics* (1916). Saussure sees language as a synchronic system of signs, that is, as a network of words and grammatical rules in place at a particular moment in time. He cuts language off from history, studying it not as it develops over the years but as it functions in the present. Essential to the operation of the linguistic system is the notion of differential interrelatedness. The units in a system take on meaning not in isolation but through their relations with other units, through the ways in which these units, though similar in certain respects, finally differ from each other: cat is cat in virtue of its difference from dog, horse, house, etc. Words do not refer to things in the world in a one-to-one, unmediated fashion; rather, they signify ideas about the world, ways of ordering and structuring it, which are generated within a relational framework.[16] Cat is a concept, produced by its differences from other concepts, through which certain physical things in the world are endowed with sense and significance, made comprehensible.

Roland Barthes, perhaps the best known and most influential of the French structuralists, draws heavily on Saussurean notions in his 1963 essay "The Structuralist Activity," an excellent summation of the structuralist vision. Capitalizing on Saussure's insight that items are meaningful only through their interrela-

INTRODUCTION

tions, Barthes asserts that for the structuralist objects acquire sense and significance in the context of general conceptual models, what he calls "paradigms."[17] For example, the planet Saturn gains its identity, its meaning and significance, not alone but in relation to all the other planets within the solar system. "What characterizes the paradigmatic object," writes Barthes, "is that it is, vis-a-vis other objects of its class, in a certain relation of affinity and dissimilarity; two units of the same paradigm must resemble each other somewhat in order that the difference which separates them be indeed evident. . . ."[18] Everything, he maintains, is a paradigmatic object of some sort; nothing, verbal or nonverbal, is meaningful outside an organized scheme of differences. That is to say, Barthes believes that reality makes sense only when conceptualized as a language. He goes on to note that one of the main tasks of the structuralist is to discover "the rules of association" (the grammar) which order and structure the differentially related units (the vocabulary) within a system.[19] Much structuralist literary criticism, in fact, consists of establishing such rules of association among elements in a given text or group of texts. For example, Tzvetan Todorov, another of the French structuralists, attempts, in a 1969 study, a grammatical analysis of the key components of Giovanni Boccaccio's *The Decameron.* As Eagleton explains, "characters are seen as nouns, their attributes as adjectives and their actions as verbs. Each story of *The Decameron* can thus be read as a kind of extended sentence, combining these units in different ways."[20] Similar scientific, linguistic dissections and orderings of texts and their component parts are carried out in American structuralist works, for example, in Gerald Prince's *A Grammar of Stories* (1973) and

Narratology: The Form and Functioning of Narrative (1982).[21]

Even as structuralism was being introduced in America, its critique was already under way in the work of a French philosopher whose ideas have proved to be more influential, whose texts have been more often cited, mined for reading strategies, and hotly contested, than perhaps any other theorist in the last thirty years: Jacques Derrida. In 1966 at a conference held at Johns Hopkins University, Derrida delivered a paper entitled "Structure, Sign and Play in the Discourse of the Human Sciences" in which he squarely attacked certain structuralist tenets and ushered in the critical school of thought which has come to be known as deconstruction.[22] In this essay, and even more clearly and in greater detail in a series of other texts—*Of Grammatology; Speech and Phenomena; Positions; Writing and Difference*—which first appeared in this country in translation in the 1970s and early 1980s, Derrida carries the Saussurean-structuralist principle that units in a system have meaning not in isolation but through their differential relations to its extreme conclusion. If the meaning—what in structuralist parlance is known as the "signified"—designated by a particular word is produced by its differences from the meanings of other words, then that meaning, Derrida argues, must be a tissue of the "traces" of those other meanings. Each signified is built out of the signifieds it differs from. Without those contrasting signifieds, it would not be what it is. This implies that, paradoxically enough, a signified is what it is not, contains within itself its opposites. There must be present in each signified other signifieds it differs from in order for that signified to be itself. Saussure and the structuralists fail to recognize this fact, Derrida thinks, by tacitly assuming the existence of unitary, separable items which can be related to each other. Derrida undermines the structuralist notion of an organized system, showing that there are no distinct, wholly separable positions to be ordered and occupied.[23] Deconstruction, in Derridean terms, is the act of detecting opposite meanings contained in a seemingly single and straightforward meaning, of scrambling established structures by demonstrating that items in those structures overlap and intercirculate.

A specific illustration will perhaps help clarify some of these notoriously complex and difficult ideas. A typical Derridean move is to identify some traditional hierarchical system—presence/absence, nature/culture, speech/writing, male/female—in which the first term has customarily been seen as superior to and the origin of the second while the second term has been viewed as secondary to and derivative of the first, and then demonstrate that, as a result of the radical instability of the terms in the system, the order of priorities can be reversed, the system deconstructed. In the case of the nature/culture hierarchy, for instance, Derrida notes that traditionally culture has been taken to be a supplement to nature: nature comes first and culture comes afterwards; culture is grounded in and added to the natural state. Derrida contends, however, that actually the concept of nature contains *within* it the concept of culture in that (1) nature is a concept produced, as are all concepts, by culture, and (2) nature is defined, its identity constituted, as that which is *not* culture. Nature is dependent upon there always already being culture before it in order for it, nature, to be what it is; it is cultural man who produces the idea of nature, and without the idea of culture as a contrast to nature, nature would not mean what it means. In short, nature comes after and is derived from culture. The system has been reversed, the hierarchy collapsed; the primary and originary term has become the secondary and derivative term, and vice versa.[24]

Such deconstructions, it is important to note, do not establish new, substitute, fixed and stable hierarchies. Just as nature contains within it the concept of culture, so does culture, Derrida would argue, contain within it the concept of nature. Culture gains its identity through its opposition to nature and would not be what it is without this contrast. Culture is dependent upon there always already being nature before it in order for culture to be what it is. The culture/nature hierarchy can be reversed just as readily as the nature/culture hierarchy. Derrida's point is that though hierarchical systems may be and routinely are set up as fixed and final, the stability and fixity of these systems are, in the end, always chimerical.[25]

In the 1970s and 1980s Derrida's ideas, though certainly opposed by many, attracted scores of followers; deconstruction became arguably the dominant school of critical thought in the United States. The leading American deconstructors—J. Hillis Miller, Joseph Riddel, Paul de Man, Barbara Johnson, Jeffrey Mehlman—developed highly original views which, though either directly grounded in or demonstrating strong affinities with Derrida's philosophy, were certainly far more than stale repetitions or mechanical applications of his principles.[26] An example of exactly what shapes deconstruction has assumed in American theory and criticism will be given in chapter one of this book, on Paul de Man.

Perhaps the only thinker whose influence on recent theory can rival that of Derrida's is Michel Foucault. Having taught for

INTRODUCTION

the bulk of his career in the history of systems of thought at the College de France, Foucault, who died in 1984, is, like Derrida, technically a philosopher rather than a literary theorist or critic per se. Foucault is best known, as Mark Poster points out, for understanding texts, both literary and nonliterary, in relation to the societies in which they were written. In such works as *The Order of Things* (1966), *The Archaeology of Knowledge* (1969), *Discipline and Punish* (1975), and Volume I of *The History of Sexuality* (1976), he argues that authors repeat and extend ideas produced by their cultures. Texts are not, as the New Critics would have it, isolated, autotelic artifacts, but rather interconnected documents reflecting communal values and views.[27] As Poster further observes, though Foucault's emphases varied through different stages in his career, generally speaking "Foucauldian readings are sensitive to the political impact of the text and the political unconscious behind the text, informing its statements and shaping its lines of enunciation."[28] That is, he concentrates on analyzing ways in which the communal ideas that texts express are shaped by the policies and principles of those in power. Unlike Derrida whose approach, at least on one common reading of his early work referred to above, is consistent with the New Criticism in that it focuses on the language of the text apart from sociohistorical contexts, Foucault claims that that language makes sense *only* in terms of historical and cultural conditions. Foucault's influence, both direct and indirect, is evident in all the theorists, with the possible exception of de Man, considered in the chapters that follow.

Deconstruction and Foucauldian analysis, as dominant and important as they surely have been, are certainly not the only approaches to have made a significant impact on American literary theory and criticism in recent years. E. D. Hirsch, for example, whose most influential book, *Validity in Interpretation* (1967), was published several years before Derrida's or Foucault's ideas became widely known, developed a popular and powerful argument for the case that a text's meaning can be equated with its author's intention. Though his stance is obviously and self-consciously at odds with the New Critical warning against the intentional fallacy, Hirsch does not, as the New Critics implicitly did, conceive of the author's meaning as necessarily single and conscious. "An author almost always means more than he is aware of meaning,"[29] Hirsch maintains. This is because what the author consciously intends is a "willed type," defined by Hirsch as "an entity which can be represented by different instances or different contents. . . ."[30] Simply put, the author's words have multiple implications, some of which he or she may be unaware of, which count as part of his or her intended meaning. Hirsch also recognizes a level of sense, which he calls "significance," that exceeds the author's meaning. "Meaning," Hirsch neatly sums up the distinction, "is that which is represented by a text; it is what the author meant by his use of a particular sign sequence. . . . Significance, on the other hand, names a relationship between that meaning and a person, or a conception, or a situation, or indeed anything imaginable."[31] Significance is Hirsch's name for the reader's input, for interpretations which, though grounded in the text, go beyond what the author could have possibly meant, consciously or unconsciously. For example, a Freudian reading of *Hamlet* would not, on Hirsch's view, yield the text's meaning; Shakespeare, who lived many years before Freud, obviously

INTRODUCTION

could not have intended his play to illustrate principles and support the vocabulary of a theory that did not exist at the time he wrote. Rather, such a reading would constitute a possible significance of the text; Shakespeare's play can be related to, shown in retrospect to support and illustrate, another author's ideas and terminology.

It would be hard to imagine a view more antithetical to Hirsch's than that of Stanley Fish, one of the most prominent and often written about American theorists in recent years. Whereas Hirsch believes that meaning is built into the text to be read out of it and that even significance is firmly anchored in the words on the page, Fish, who makes no meaning-significance distinction, believes that *all* the text's meaning comes from outside the text and is read into it. Whereas Hirsch thinks that meaning can be equated with authorial intention and that significance is directly derived from that intention, Fish contends that everything a text means comes entirely from the reader, that the author's intention is, for all practical purposes, beside the point.

In perhaps his best-known book, *Is There a Text in This Class? The Authority of Interpretive Communities* (1980), Fish argues, in a series of loosely connected essays, that readers make sense of texts by filtering them through communally constructed and held interpretive strategies. More specifically, readers always come to texts equipped with methods for understanding them. For example, one may approach a text from a New Critical perspective, or a structuralist perspective, or a deconstructionist perspective. The reader projects that strategy upon the text, constituting for it a meaning consistent with the strategy. One can never, Fish insists, place oneself outside all strategies and, in

New Critical fashion, read the text "objectively": "one hears an utterance within, and not as preliminary to determining, a knowledge of its purposes and concerns [as defined by a particular interpretive strategy], and . . . to so hear it is already to have assigned it a shape and given it a meaning."[32] Nor may one make up an entirely private interpretive strategy: "an individual's assumptions and opinions [the interpretive strategy the reader invokes] are not 'his own.' . . . *he* is not their origin . . . rather, it is their prior availability which delimits in advance the paths that his consciousness can possibly take."[33] Fishean reading, in sum, is always a wholly biased, perspectival activity, dictated by modes of understanding held in conjunction with other readers.

In the same essay from which the above quotations are taken, "Is There a Text in This Class?," Fish gives a concrete instance to illustrate his generalizations. Citing an actual encounter he witnessed while on the faculty at Johns Hopkins University, Fish notes that the question "Is there a text in this class?" means radically different things to a particular professor and one of his students. The student, who puts this question to the professor shortly after attending his course for the first time, intends her words as a query about whether or not the professor believes in the objective existence, the inherent meaningfulness, of texts. Having taken classes from Fish, she wonders if her teacher operates under the assumption that literary works are anything more than mere pretexts for Fishean-like acts of readerly constitution. The professor, on the other hand, takes "text" to mean textbook; he thinks the student, uncertain of the course requirements, is asking if a particular anthology will be used in his class. He thus responds to her question with what to her is an inadequate, confusing answer: "'Yes, it's the *Norton Anthology of Literature.*'" These different interpretations are possible, Fish concludes, not because "Is there a text in this class?" contains two distinct meanings, but rather because two distinct meanings are foisted upon the question from outside. The student, steeped in Fishean methodology, makes the words mean one thing, while the professor, locked into assumptions about the kinds of questions students normally ask at the beginning of the semester, makes the words mean something entirely different.[34]

One of the most controversial and idiosyncratic theorists on the contemporary scene is Harold Bloom. Though often categorized as a full-blooded deconstructor, he actually falls somewhere between deconstruction and the school of criticism with which Fish is frequently affiliated, reader-response. Bloom shares the deconstructors' fascination with subversive, destabilizing interpretations, but he sees meaning, somewhat like Fish, as coming from outside the text rather than, as deconstructors see it, solely from within it. Bloom's focus, which he develops in a series of books including *The Anxiety of Influence* (1973), *A Map of Misreading* (1975), and *Agon: Towards a Theory of Revisionism* (1982), is literary history. Literature, which for him includes theory and criticism, is generated through critical influence, by a writer's creative revision of his or her predecessors' works. Such revision Bloom calls "misreading," noting that its purpose is to clear "imaginative space" so that the newcomer author will have room to assert his or her originality[35]. The young artist creates his or her work by attempting to improve upon, to rewrite in fresh and original terms, the plots, themes, and images of past greats. Bloom's theory is Freudian in that it casts authors in the role of ambitious sons who anxiously desire to eliminate the powerful, oppressive, and seductive presence of their literary fathers in order to establish their own identities and dominance.

It is important to note that on Bloom's view the poet, which is the term he uses for all types of writers, need not have actually read the precursor text by which his or her work is influenced. A poem is a response to some "central poem by an indubitable precursor, even if the ephebe [latecomer poet] *never read* that poem."[36] This is because, as Peter de Bolla explains and commentators frequently fail to recognize, the Bloomian text functions *as if* it were the author's conscious revision of another text, even if such conscious intent does not exist. Bloom, in effect, posits two different notions of "poet." It is the poet as a voice incarnated in the text that may always be seen as jealously responding to the voice in some prior text. The poet as a living human being, who creates the textual voice, may or may not consciously experience the anxiety of influence exemplified by the poet incarnated in his or her text.[37]

Any number of other theorists and schools of thought might be cited to fill out the field in which the subjects of this book operate, but the few mentioned here suffice to establish at least a sketchy context for the work of de Man, Gates, Showalter, Greenblatt, Said, and Rorty. With the exception of de Man, who died in 1983, all those featured in the chapters that follow are alive today, in 1995, and making important contributions. Except for de Man, a deconstructor, all focus, in one way or another, on the role culture and history play in

INTRODUCTION

the production of both literary and nonliterary meaning. This is not to say that only de Man bears affinities with and reflects the influence of those theorists, some of whom are noted above, who ignore history and culture. Very few critics writing since 1970 or so have been able, for instance, to escape the sweeping, powerful impress of Derrida and deconstruction; none of the six presented in this book have. Nor have the ideas of theorists writing in the early part of this century been completely lost in the present. New Critical emphases on close reading and the ambiguities of literary language, for example, filtered their way into American deconstruction, which, in turn, has filtered its way, in mutated and truncated forms, into the six subjects of this book. Contemporary theory is a complicated fabric of crisscrossing and tangled threads, no one of which can be entirely separated from the others.

Many recent theorists have argued that theory and criticism are arts, not easily or clearly distinguishable from the texts they comment upon. The way one interprets a text creates, to a significant degree, the text one interprets. For example, Fish turns each text into the particular meanings different interpretive communities project upon it, while Bloom makes every text a creative revision of some previous work. "All criticism is prose poetry,"[38] writes Bloom. And Geoffrey Hartman declares, echoing Bloom: "reading at its closest leads to the counter-fabrication of writing. . . . We cannot gain real insight into an artist or ourselves by pure contemplation, only by the contemplation that making (*poesis*) enables."[39]

None of the theorists covered in this book merely describes, in a submissive fashion, what is already there, either in literature or other cultural documents; rather, each helps produce—"counter-fabricates," to use Hartman's term—the texts he or she studies. What follows, then, will be an introduction to the "prose poems" of a few of the most prominent theorists/critics working today.

CHAPTER TWO

Paul de Man
Deconstruction

The son of Magdalena de Braey and Robert de Man, a manufacturer, Paul de Man was born in Antwerp, Belgium, on December 6, 1919. From 1949 to 1951 he taught French literature at Bard College in New York, after having received his Candidature from the University of Brussels in 1942. In 1958 he graduated from Harvard with an M.A., and two years later he earned his Ph.D., also from Harvard. Subsequently, he taught at Cornell (1960–67), Johns Hopkins (1967–70), and Yale (1970–83). De Man died of cancer on December 21, 1983.[1]

Recent revelations concerning de Man's past, which he kept secret until his death, have made his life as much a topic of discussion, among scholars and popular press journalists alike, as his theoretical writings. As David Lehman observes in *Signs of the Times: Deconstruction and the Fall of Paul de Man* (1991), during the 1970s and into the 1980s deconstruction was the most important, influential, and controversial school of critical thought in America, and Paul de Man was "America's archdeacon of deconstruction."[2] Working at Yale with other deconstructive illuminati such as Jacques Derrida, J. Hillis Miller, and Geoffrey Hartman, de Man became, in Frank Kermode's words, "the most celebrated member of the world's most celebrated literature school."[3] By the time of his death in 1983, he had acquired an almost cultlike following, his fame as a powerful and original interpreter of texts being rivaled by his reputation as a kind, engaging, generous, and humane teacher and friend.[4]

Then, on December 1, 1987, *The New York Times* ran a headline on the first page of the second section: "Yale Scholar's Articles Found in Nazi Paper."[5] A student named Ortwin de Graef, who was preparing a doctoral thesis on de Man, discovered a number of essays de Man had written in his early twenties for the pro-Hitler Belgian publication *Le Soir,* the most widely circulated newspaper in the country during the German occupation.[6] These columns, now collected in a volume entitled *Wartime Journalism, 1940–1942* (1989), "advanced the Nazis' cultural agenda in ways small and large."[7] In the the most damning and inflammatory of the pieces, "The Jews and Contemporary Literature," de Man judges Jewish authors to be second- rate and calls for the establishment of a colony separate from the rest of Europe to which all Jews should be exiled.[8]

Though the discovery of this youthful journalism must obviously alter the perception of Paul de Man the person, toppling him from the pedestal upon which many had placed him, does it affect the value and status of his work, change the meaning and significance of his theory and criticism? Some have answered yes. Because of the nature of the claims he makes about language, literature, and history, it is possible to see de Man's theories as a vast cover-up operation for his crimes, as views tacitly designed to justify forgetting, and even altering, a distasteful past. Lehman's book and others, such as David H. Hirsch's *The Deconstruction of Literature: Criticism After Auschwitz* (1991), along with a number of essays, several of which are collected in *Responses: On Paul de Man's Wartime Journalism*

PAUL de MAN: DECONSTUCTION

(1989), make this case. But de Man also has his apologists. For example, Jacques Derrida's *Memories: For Paul de Man* (1986) and several of the essays in *Responses* mount various defenses of the Yale scholar and his work. It perhaps makes most sense to see de Man's theories as instruments that *might* be used in the cause of some devious, covert amnesty project but that also might have entirely innocent purposes, wholly devoid of nefarious implications.

At the heart of the stance de Man develops is irony; his version of deconstruction is best understood in terms of this concept. In order to discern the uses de Man makes of irony and its connection with deconstruction, it is first important to have a clear understanding of what irony is. Irony always involves conflicting layers of meaning, layers which are interconnected and mutually undo each other. The ironic utterance double-talks, says opposite things simultaneously. It overtly states one meaning and covertly expresses another. In a 1980 interview with Robert Moynihan, de Man explains his notion of irony, couching this explanation in terms of authorial intention. "There's irony when language starts to say things you didn't think it was saying," he argues, "when words acquire meanings way beyond the one you think you are controlling and start saying things that go against your own quest for meaning or admitted intention."[9] To say that irony undermines a text's explicit, overt meaning is not to say that it cancels that meaning altogether. Though the ironic utterance conveys senses contrary to the one the author intended, it expresses the intended sense as well. When, for example, at the beginning of *Oedipus the King* Oedipus declares "not one is sick as I,"[10] the irony arises from the subversion of the surface meaning which Oedipus intends—that no one in the kingdom is more sickened than he is over the suffering caused by the plague and famine that have struck Thebes—by a hidden and deviant meaning which we as readers, with a knowledge of the play's conclusion, realize his words sponsor—that no one in the kingdom is so sick as to have slept with his mother and killed his father, as Oedipus has done.

Irony depends upon there being a single and stable meaning to destabilize and rupture. Unless it is possible to establish a clear and unambiguous interpretation for a particular text, then it is obviously impossible to show that such an interpretation is contradicted by an implicit, opposite meaning: Oedipus's irony is as dependent upon his own, unequivocal interpretation of his words as it is upon the contrary implications the reader derives from them. As de Man puts it, "if it is true that [ironic] texts always undo readings, it is equally true that texts constitute meanings." He knows that irony "necessarily produces meanings but that [it] also undoes what it produces."[11] De Man seizes upon this notion of irony and declares that *all* language is potentially ironic. If carefully scrutinized, each utterance can be shown to convey distinct meanings that contradict each other. De Man's contention is that whenever one uses words, one necessarily loses command of one's intention. Whether one realizes it or not, one always says something more and other than what one means to say. Every "claim of control" made by an author, de Man asserts, "can always be shown to be unwarranted—one can show that the claim of control is a mistake, that there are elements in the text that are not controlled, that it is always possible to read the text against the overt claim of control."[12]

PAUL de MAN: DECONSTUCTION

De Man's interpretations of literary, critical, and philosophical texts repeatedly attest to the fact that irony is everywhere present. De Manian deconstruction, then, is simply the act of detecting and accounting for irony. To deconstruct is to explain how and why a particular author loses control of his or her intended meaning. It is to demonstrate that a particular text, which has traditionally been interpreted as having a single, clear-cut sense, actually sponsors this traditional sense *plus* other, opposite senses. Texts, in effect, dismantle themselves, de Man reveals; their language, when closely examined, falls apart into contradictory meanings. The deconstructor merely uncovers the hidden power and results of the disruptive logic inherent in language.

Such critics as Walter Jackson Bate[13] and M. H. Abrams[14] who accuse de Man and other deconstructors of nihilism, of abandoning the possibility of definite truths and clear communication, are only half right. De Man, following the paradoxical logic of irony, denies the clarity and certainty of precisely those communications and truths he posits as clear and certain. Much of the appeal of his approach lies in its heretical power to complicate and question, while at the same time preserving, that which has previously been viewed as unequivocally true.

Of course, de Man's own language is not exempt from duplicity, from stating a clear and certain meaning which can be deconstructed, and he knows it. When in the Moynihan interview de Man says "*any* [italics added] reading of a text can be put in question, 'ironized,' if you wish, by another reading,"[15] he is implicitly recognizing that his own ironic interpretations of texts can themselves be shown to be ironic, to contain implicit meanings which subvert their stated intentions. Thus there is no problem, as certain critics such as Frank Lentricchia have assumed, with de Man asserting authoritatively and unequivocally the correctness of his interpretations and theory even though those interpretations and that theory illustrate and assert that no interpretation or theory is authoritatively or unequivocally correct.[16] For de Man to use words to convey a clear and single meaning, in spite of the fact that he knows that all words, his own included, can be shown to contain contradictory senses, is for him to act entirely in keeping with his theory. As William Ray observes, "for the ironic reader, belief is always accompanied by the belief that what one believes cannot be the full story: there is always something further, something more, to be understood in understanding."[17]

The best way to see how these general principles play themselves out in practice is, of course, to examine specific de Manian texts. De Man's first major work was *Blindness and Insight: Essays in the Rhetoric of Contemporary Criticism,* originally published in 1971 and reissued in an expanded form in 1983. This book, which in its 1983 version contains two forewords, twelve essays, and two appendices, is as the title suggests a work of metacriticism, a collection of interpretations of other literary critics' theories and interpretations. As de Man notes in the first, original foreword, the selections were originally "written for specific occasions—conferences, lectures, homages" over a period of several years.[18] He denies that these pieces follow or illustrate any "pre-established theories of literary interpretation" (vii). Nonetheless, he does explicitly identify a central theme which unites them: "in all of them [the figures whose work he analyzes] a paradoxical discrepancy appears between the general statements they make about the nature of literature (statements on which they base their critical methods) and the actual results of their interpretations" (ix). That is, de Man continues, "their findings about the structure of texts contradict the general conception that they use as their model" (ix). These critics' books and essays, in short, are ironic, and can be deconstructed.

De Man's claim is that critics routinely set up abstract principles dictating a particular range of meanings that literary works will have, but when they actually apply those principles to specific works, those works turn out to have meanings that fall outside that range, that contradict the principles. For example, a particular marxist's assertion that all literary texts reflect the economic conditions of the societies in which they were written might be shown to be at odds with his or her application of this theory to a specific text. The critic's interpretation, when scrutinized, actually disproves, ironically enough, his or her claim that the text reflects economic realities. Critics, like Oedipus, are oblivious to their irony; it is de Man the reader, not those critics he reads, who ferrets out the contradictions. De Man is able to see what the critics cannot see, that their most insightful interpretations are made possible by theories with which those interpretations are at odds. It is because the marxist interpreter is blind to the contradictions between his or her theoretical pronouncements and the readings of specific texts those pronouncements generate that he or she is able so freely and convincingly to produce the readings. "Not only do they [critics] remain unaware of this discrepancy [between critical findings and theoretical claims]," argues de Man, "but they seem to thrive on it and owe their best insights to the assumptions these insights disprove" (ix).

De Man exposes and describes this pattern of blindness and insight throughout the twelve essays of his book, which cover such figures as Ludwig Binswanger, Georg Lukacs, Maurice Blanchot, Georges Poulet, and Jacques Derrida. "Form and Intent in the American New Criticism," the second essay in the book, is a particularly lucid and straightforward example of his tactics. Here de Man identifies a discrepancy between the theory and practice of the New Critics. The gist of the argument is presented midway through the essay. De Man writes: "As it refines its interpretations more and more, American [New] criticism does not discover a single meaning, but a plurality of significations that can be radically opposed to each other. Instead of revealing a continuity affiliated with the coherence of the natural world, it takes us into a discontinuous world of reflective irony and ambiguity. Almost in spite of itself, it pushes the interpretative process so far that the analogy between the organic world and the language of poetry finally explodes. This unitarian criticism finally becomes a criticism of ambiguity, an ironic reflection on the absence of the unity it had postulated" (28).

On the one hand, de Man maintains, the New Critics theorize that the effective poem unifies opposed concepts into a harmonious, coherent whole. They see the poem as analogous to a natural, animate object: just as a tree is one thing that has several different parts—limbs, leaves, roots, etc.—so does the good poem form one meaning from distinct ideas. On the other hand, de Man observes that the New Critics affirm through the specific interpretations generated by their theory that texts are not unified wholes at all but rather confluences of opposed concepts that finally cannot be integrated. He claims that the analogy with the natural world is invalid; poems are nothing like seamless, living organisms. Christopher Norris succinctly sums up de Man's position: "Their [the New Critics'] obsession with 'organic' form was undermined by those very 'ambiguities' and 'tensions' which they sought out in order to praise, and so contain, them."[19]

De Man does not give a specific, detailed example to illustrate his argument, but such an example can easily be imagined. In "The Language of Paradox," the prominent New Critic Cleanth Brooks attempts to show how Wordsworth's sonnet, "Composed Upon Westminster Bridge," yokes disparate concepts. The poem, he asserts, hinges on the ascription of natural qualities to man-made objects. For example, Wordsworth describes the city of London as possessing the same beauty that majestic mountain ranges and fields of flowers have. The poet causes the reader to see, in Brooks's words, that "man-made London is part of nature too. . . ."[20] The point of the poem, Brooks concludes, is to fuse the distinct ideas of nature and civilization, to demonstrate the paradox that these apparently different realms are really one.

De Man's contention would be that Brooks is imposing a unity that does not exist. This New Critic's attempt to equate civilization with nature in Wordsworth's sonnet, De Man would argue, actually calls attention to the irreconcilable difference between these two realms; there must be, at some fundamental level, a concept of civilization separate from the concept of nature in order for the former to appear to have the qualities and be a part of the latter. Brooks identifies analogies the poet draws between nature and civilization, analogies which, like all analogies, do not show that one thing is just the same thing as another, but rather implicitly highlight the radical distinction between two, different things in the very act of comparing them. What Brooks has done, quite unintentionally, is produce an interpretation that proves that opposite ideas do *not* cohere in Wordsworth's poem to form a unified, organic whole.

As de Man specifies in the introduction to *Blindness and Insight,* the critic's interpretation is generated by a theory with which the interpretation is at odds. Brooks unwittingly establishes the ultimate irreconcilability of distinct concepts in "Composed Upon Westminster Bridge" as a result of his New Critical interpretive model that prompts the identification of these concepts but calls for, and tries to force, their conflation. In other words, de Man shows in "Form and Intent in the American New Criticism" that what he asserts in the Moynihan interview to be true for all authors holds in the specific case of the New Critics: they lose control over their intentions; their texts are ironic in that the interpretations of particular poems presented in these texts contradict the premises of their theory. De Man's deconstruction of the New Criticism consists of his recognition and analysis of this irony.

De Man continues this prying apart of critical texts in the sixth essay in *Blindness and Insight,* "The Literary Self as Origin: The Work of Georges Poulet." By focusing on contradictions in the positions Poulet, a contemporary French critic, formulates, de Man is able to reveal an irony inherent in the nature of all literary expression. Poulet argues, de Man claims, that the critic's job is to commune with and communicate to the reader the self of the author whose texts he or she is analyzing. That is, Poulet believes the literary text transparently conveys the unique and original consciousness of its author and that the good critic can know and then transparently convey this consciousness to the reader through his or her criticism. Poulet's critic, in de Man's words, becomes "a passageway (*lieu de passage*) for another person's thought" (96). The author who "presides over the invention of a work is present in this work as a unique and absolute source" (96), and when the sensitive critic reads the work, he or she is able to "coincide entirely with this source in the act of critical identification. . . ." (96).

Poulet, however, fails to practice what he preaches, de Man maintains. In his own criticism, he does not merely serve up the subjectivity of another; instead, he does things to and with the texts he reads. Rather than being a passive "passageway," he is an active analyst. De Man's contention is that Poulet's criticism, like all good criticism, comments upon and creatively interprets texts, never attempting exactly to reproduce the consciousness which informs and is the original source of the literary work being analyzed. As de Man puts it, Poulet "participates, much more than he claims to do, in the problematic possibility of their [the texts] elaboration" (97).

This participation and elaboration stem in large part from his questioning of the very self which he declares is unproblematically contained in and immediately available for extraction from the text. According to de Man, when Poulet actually interprets literary works, he implicitly "undermine[s] the stability of the subject" by recognizing a fundamental difference between that subject and the language through which it expresses itself in the work (97). More specifically, Poulet demonstrates that the author's self cannot coincide with literary language because that language is a system of socially made and held concepts that is something other than the private self. When an author writes, he or she is not directly communicating his or her living, unique being but is instead retrospectively translating it into the transpersonal medium of linguistic, literary conventions. What Poulet inadvertently discovers is that a text is only a "form of a written language that relates, in its turn, to other written languages in the history of literature and criticism" (98).

De Man's deconstruction of Poulet consists of his identification of a fundamental irony in the French critic's work. Poulet's explicit theory, which posits the possibility of the critic communing with and conveying an author's private self, leads into reflections upon the difference between such an authorial self and the language it uses. These reflections, in turn, unwittingly call the theory into question; if an author cannot immediately convey his or her consciousness through words, then it is obviously impossible for the critic to commune with and then communicate that consciousness. Through this deconstruction, de Man in effect identifies an irony inherent in *every* author-text relationship. Texts are written by authors as expressions of their innermost beings, but the medium of expression—language— circumvents the possibility of any such direct expression.

The arguments de Man presents in "The Literary Self as Origin" and which he reiterates in various ways throughout his texts are ones that might be used to argue that there is a connection between his Nazi-tainted youth and mature literary theory. Is it not convenient for someone who would like to deny allegiances expressed in print to maintain that there is a distance and difference between the actual, living self and the words it produces, that the two cannot be equated? Is it not convenient for someone who wants to escape past mistakes preserved in texts to concoct a view grounded in the notion that texts are inherently ironic, that they always say things one does not intend for them to say? Such a theory would allow de Man to deny that his anti-Semitic proclamations mean just what they appear to mean. "In converting language into the fated instrument of 'untruth,'" David H. Hirsch argues, "de Man elevated deception to a high art."[21] As already noted, however, de Man's theory does not have to be interpreted this way. His essay on Poulet, like his other essays that express similar ideas, can be read for its manifest content, as a deconstruction of another critic's criticism that has nothing to do with excusing his personal past.

In "The Rhetoric of Temporality," perhaps the best known of the pieces in the second, revised edition of *Blindness and Insight,* de Man extends the argument, central to "The Literary Self as Origin," that there is a fundamental difference between language and that which it represents. Carefully distinguishing symbol from allegory, de Man rejects as illusion the former, which supposedly unites language and reality in a seamless whole, and champions as authentic the latter, which calls attention to the gulf between words and the things in the world they refer to. De Man maintains that nineteenth-century Romantic writers and their modern commentators who believe that it is possible directly to convey external nature and lived experience through symbols are deluded; the poet's language, even when the poet or critic fails to recognize it, actually functions as allegory, transforming external nature and lived experience into that which they are not in themselves, namely, linguistic concepts. Critical and poetic texts that argue, either explicitly or implicitly, for the existence and superior value of the symbol, de Man demonstrates, undermine themselves by inadvertently revealing symbols to be allegories in disguise (187–228).

The details of this analysis of the Romantic notion of the symbol are fascinating and complex. But it is not necessary to rehearse these details in order to discern that the point of "The Rhetoric of Temporality," like that of "Form and Intent in the New Criticism" and "The Literary Self as Origin," is to disclose ways in which authors contradict themselves, to show how their texts deconstruct. As already noted, de Man is aware that his deconstructions can themselves be deconstructed, that he also contradicts himself. He knows that just as he is able to identify blindnesses in the insights of others, so might others detect blind spots in his own revelations. As Jonathan Culler records, de Man, in an essay about Rousseau, explicitly admits to just such blindness and contradiction: "'needless to say, this new interpretation [his deconstruction of Rousseau] will, in its own turn, be caught in its own form of blindness.'"[22] The irony of de Man's ironic project is that the claims he makes must be, in keeping with his theory, subject to ironic dismantling.

The only other book de Man published in his lifetime was *Allegories of Reading: Figural Language in Rousseau, Nietzsche, Rilke and Proust,* which first appeared in 1979. Divided into two parts, the first entitled "Rhetoric" and the second "Rousseau," this collection of twelve essays, several of which were originally published in journals some years earlier, provides deconstructive

PAUL de MAN: DECONSTUCTION

readings of Rousseau primarily—six of the twelve focus on the French philosopher—and, as the subtitle suggests, Nietzsche, Rilke, and Proust as well. De Man opens the preface to this book by noting that *"Allegories of Reading* started out as a historical study and ended up as a theory of reading. I began to read Rousseau seriously in preparation for a historical reflection on Romanticism and found myself unable to progress beyond local difficulties of interpretation."[23] As in *Blindness and Insight,* de Man demonstrates, this time with an emphasis on the ambiguities generated by rhetoric, that language does not communicate single, stable meanings but rather always signifies a tangle of interconnected and contradictory senses. In *Allegories of Reading,* Raman Selden observes, de Man "develops a 'rhetorical' type of deconstruction already begun in *Blindness and Insight."* He outlines a theory of interpretation that "denies the possibility of a straightforwardly literal or referential use of language."[24]

The best known piece in the collection is the first, "Semiology and Rhetoric." Probably because it is one of the most accessible of all de Man's texts, this essay is frequently reprinted, often serving as the representative de Manian piece in anthologies of contemporary criticism. Here de Man gives two very specific, very clear and simple examples of deconstruction, drawing out the implications of his procedure and explaining what it is about language that enables his moves. Though there are certainly significant differences among his texts, the model for interpretation he establishes in "Semiology and Rhetoric" might serve as a general model for the theory and practice of interpretation underlying all of de Man's work, including the essays, already reviewed, in *Blindness and Insight.*

The first of the deconstructions is carried out on a bit of dialogue from the 1970s television comedy, *All in the Family*. Upon being questioned by his wife, Edith, as to whether he wants his bowling shoes laced over or under, Archie Bunker asks "'What's the difference?'" "Being a reader of sublime simplicity," de Man reports, "his wife replies by patiently explaining the difference between lacing over and lacing under, whatever this may be. . . " (9). Archie responds to Edith's response with anger and frustration. His question "did not ask for difference but means instead 'I don't give a damn what the difference is'" (9). The two are at odds over how a particular text—"'What's the difference?'"—should be interpreted. Archie intends his question rhetorically, but Edith reads it literally.

The most conspicuous implication of this interchange, one which de Man does not explicitly name but obviously intends, is that *all* language, be it that of literature, criticism, television programs, or anything else, works the same way. He uses the Bunker text to illustrate principles of interpretation which apply to texts in general, not just to this one. What are these principles? Perhaps the most evident, fundamental, and least controversial is that it is always possible to read texts in multiple ways, that texts can and do have more than one meaning. De Man makes it clear in his analysis of Archie's question that neither Archie's nor Edith's reading is *the* correct one: "it is impossible to decide . . . which of the two meanings . . . prevails" (10). Both interpretations, he maintains, are equally legitimate and correct.

This, however, does not mean that the two interpretations are not in conflict with or do not compete against each other. To the contrary, de Man highlights the fact that to assert one meaning is

PAUL de MAN: DECONSTUCTION

to undermine and deny the other: "The same grammatical pattern [in Archie's text] engenders two meanings that are mutually exclusive: the literal meaning asks for the concept (difference) whose existence is denied by the figurative meaning" (9). A second principle of interpretation, one more subtle and provocative than the first, that comes out of this example is that to read a text one way is to ignore or fail to recognize that it also sponsors some other interpretation that subverts that reading. In other words, as de Man maintains in the Moynihan interview, texts are subject to ironic interpretation; they are double (at least) voiced, saying contradictory things simultaneously. Meaning never finally settles into a single assertion but instead is fractured and multiple, circulating among opposed senses.

A final, corollary principle that the Archie text illustrates, one asserted abstractly in the Moynihan interview and demonstrated concretely throughout *Blindness and Insight* and *Allegories of Reading,* is that authors cannot control their meanings. What the words of a text imply go way beyond any single intent the author may have projected. Archie's impatience with Edith's reply, de Man asserts, "reveals his despair when confronted with a structure of linguistic meaning that he cannot control and that holds the discouraging prospect of an infinity of similar future confusions . . ."(10). It is not that authors can never say what they mean; rather, it is that they can never say *only* what they mean. Authors, that is, never say what they mean without also saying something other than what they mean, which falsifies what they mean to say.

De Man, in order to fortify his case, reiterates these lessons from the Bunker text in relation to a second text, the last line—

"How can we know the dancer from the dance?"—of William Butler Yeats's poem "Among School Children." The traditional, usual interpretation of this line, de Man observes, is that the dancer cannot be distinguished from the dance. Yeats's text asserts, in the form of a rhetorical question, the impossibility of separating actor from act, form from content. In de Man's own words, "the line is usually interpreted as stating, with the increased emphasis of a rhetorical device, the potential unity between form and experience, between creator and creation" (11). However, the question can also be construed, de Man insists, in another, counter way. It can be "read literally as meaning that, since the dancer and the dance are not the same, it might be useful, perhaps even desperately necessary—for the question can be given a ring of urgency, 'Please tell me, how *can* I know the dancer from the dance'—to tell them apart" (12). That is, the question can be taken as a disguised assertion that actor and act, form and content *can,* in fact, be separated, that each can be known as a distinct identity.

The two interpretations, de Man argues, are both legitimate, cannot be reconciled, subvert each other, and imply that a text's meaning always exceeds any single authorial intention. Writes de Man: "Neither can we say, as was already the case in the first example [the Bunker text], that the poem simply has two meanings that exist side by side. The two readings have to engage each other in direct confrontation, for the one reading is precisely the error denounced by the other and has to be undone by it. Nor can we in any way make a valid decision as to which of the readings can be given priority over the other; none can exist in the other's absence" (12). Just as in the case of the Archie Bunker text, the author's language is shown to be ironic, saying opposite, contradictory things simultaneously.

At the outset of "Semiology and Rhetoric," de Man explains that it is because language is thoroughly rhetorical that it generates multiple, contradictory meanings. "Rhetoric," he proclaims, "opens up vertiginous possibilities of referential aberration" (10). By rhetoric, de Man does not mean the skillful use of words to persuade, a common definition of the term, but rather he alludes to words' figural capacity, to their ability, as he defines figurality, to refer to different meanings at once, each meaning being an "error" in relation to the others (8). For example, "hit the books" is a clearly figural or rhetorical phrase whose literal meaning, to physically strike the books, is at odds with, a mistake in relation to, its figurative meaning, to study hard. "Hit the books" sponsors these opposite meanings simultaneously. In other words rhetoric is, for de Man, synonymous with irony. It is certainly ironic that when one gives the instruction to hit the books one means something radically other than what one literally says. Irony becomes the preeminent rhetorical device, which infects and forms the basis of all forms of figurality. De Man's semiology—his study of linguistic signs—leads him to the conclusion that not just obvious cases, such as "hit the books," but *all* utterances, including the Bunker and Yeats lines, are ultimately rhetorical, which is to say ironic (10).

The dismantling of truth claims through the power of rhetoric takes a particularly interesting turn in the sixth essay of *Allegories of Reading,* "Rhetoric of Tropes (Nietzsche)." Here de Man turns Friedrich Nietzsche's theory of rhetoric, a theory essentially the same as but with different emphases than the one

UNDERSTANDING CONTEMPORARY LITERARY THEORY

de Man relies on in "Semiology and Rhetoric," against itself. He quotes the nineteenth-century German philosopher as claiming that "'no such thing as an unrhetorical, "natural" language exists. . . . Language is rhetoric'" (105). De Man then explains that rhetoric, as Nietzsche defines it, signifies the power of words to mean something other than what they actually, directly pick out. Rhetoric is Nietzsche's name for a word's ability to suggest a metaphorical meaning that covers and stands in for its literal, authentic referent (106). Nietzsche illustrates this concept of rhetoric in a passage in *On Truth and Lie in the Extra-Moral Sense*. Here he asserts that the traditional, Western "idea of individuation, of the human subject as a privileged viewpoint, is a mere metaphor by means of which man protects himself from his insignificance by forcing his own interpretation of the world upon the entire universe, substituting a human-centered set of meanings that is reassuring to his vanity for a set of meanings that reduces him to being a mere transitory accident in the cosmic order" (111). That is, Western man has come to define the self as the center of creation, as a supremely important being capable of ordering and controlling the world. Nietzsche's claim is that this definition is rhetorical in that it swaps a comforting fiction for a disturbing, contrary reality. The truth is, despite what our language suggests to the contrary, that man is not the center and controller of things; he is an insignificant, transitory blip at the mercy of a universe beyond his mastery. Nietzsche is attempting to expose the deceptions of language, revealing the false, metaphorical sense of the self that has hidden and come to substitute for its true, authentic, literal meaning.

There is a crippling problem with this argument, De Man

maintains. He perceptively points out that "the text [Nietzsche's] that asserts this annihilation of the self is not consumed, because it still sees itself as the center that produces the affirmation. . . . Making the language that denies the self into a center rescues the self linguistically at the same time that it asserts its insignificance. . ." (111–12). In other words, Nietzsche inadvertently affirms the meaning of the self he sets out to refute in the very act of refuting it. His authorial self, the voice of the narrator in his text, orders and controls the world, establishes itself as a center and maker of meaning, by magisterially constructing from language a coherent, meaningful definition of the self—a key component of the world—as an insignificant, transitory blip incapable of ordering and controlling the world.

What De Man does, in short, is deconstruct Nietzsche. He shows that Nietzsche's rhetorical analysis of the language of the self is necessarily undermined by the rhetoric of the language in which Nietzsche conducts that analysis. More specifically, de Man argues that since all words, as Nietzsche prescribes, are rhetorical, then Nietzsche's words must be rhetorical as well. His words too must substitute a metaphorical, deceptive meaning for a literal, true referent. And indeed they do. Nietzsche replaces the authentic idea of the self as central and fully capable of shaping the world with a falsifying notion of the self as insignificant and incapable of shaping the world. His own words, as noted, establish the illegitimacy of his substitution; the speaker of those words *is* a self that orders and shapes reality, thus such selves obviously do exist, contrary to what he explicitly argues. De Man, in sum, shows *On Truth and Lie in the Extra-Moral Sense* to be the same sort of text as Archie Bunker's, Yeats's, and the critics' in *Blindness and Insight:* profoundly ironic.

Several other collections of de Man's essays appeared after his death, including *The Rhetoric of Romanticism* (1984), *The Resistance to Theory* (1986), *Critical Writings: 1953–1978* (1989), and *Aesthetic Ideology* (1992). The latter of these, Cynthia Chase notes, gathers "rhetorical readings of texts of Immanuel Kant, Friedrich Schiller, and G. W. F. Hegel . . . focused on the concept of the sublime and on the function and status of the category of the aesthetic."[25] *Critical Writings,* as the cover of the paperback edition advertises, "brings together twenty-five essays and reviews heretofore scattered in American, British, and French publications, eight of them translated into English for the first time." These pieces, most of which were originally published before 1970, engage the works of such diverse writers as Michel Eyquem de Montaigne, Jean-Jacques Rousseau, John Keats, Johann Wolfgang von Goethe, Charles Baudelaire, Stéphane Mallarmé, Jean-Paul Sartre, André Gide, and Albert Camus. *The Resistance to Theory* consists of an interview with de Man and five essays, ranging from an analysis of the ironies of translation to a consideration of the contradictions built into every work of literary theory.

The longest of these four posthumous books, and in many respects the most interesting, is *The Rhetoric of Romanticism.* Gathered here are ten essays, treating such Romantic authors as Percy Bysshe Shelley, Heinrich Wilhelm von Kleist, William Wordsworth, and Frederich Hölderlin. The earliest of these pieces—a lengthy segment from de Man's dissertation on Yeats—dates back to the 1950s, while the most recent were written in the 1980s, two of them having been produced shortly before his death, specifically for this volume. Christopher Norris has argued that one of the principal aims of all de Man's works is to expose the fallacies of aesthetic ideology, the assumption that poetic language can transparently and directly mirror reality.[26] This aim is especially obvious and well executed in *The Rhetoric of Romanticism* where de Man time and again shows, even as he does in "The Rhetoric of Temporality," how Romantic writers implicitly highlight the difference between nature and the words they use to describe it.

It would be interesting and informative to examine all the essays individually in de Man's last books, as well as the pieces from *Blindness and Insight* and *Allegories of Reading* not considered here, but space obviously does not permit such a comprehensive investigation. The analyses of the de Man texts that have been presented in this chapter at least touch on, if not exhaustively plumb, many of his major concerns and approaches. Perhaps the only way to do full justice to his complex and original work is to read it in the thorough, meticulous, deconstructive manner he recommends reading all texts. Such a reading, as de Man's theory itself suggests, would, however, be endless.

CHAPTER THREE

Henry Louis Gates, Jr.
Black Studies

Henry Louis Gates, Jr., is W. E. B. DuBois Professor of the Humanities and chairman of the African American Studies department at Harvard University. Born in Keyser, West Virginia, on September 16, 1950, Gates received his B.A. from Yale University in 1973 and his M.A. (1974) and Ph.D. (1979) from Cambridge. In 1981 he was awarded a MacArthur Prize fellowship.[1] Praised in *The New York Times Book Review* as "one of the best-known scholars and most eloquent advocates of African-American literature,"[2] Gates has published scores of essays in leading journals, edited anthologies and collections of criticism, and written several books. Some of the texts he has edited include *Black Literature and Literary Theory* (1984), *"Race," Writing, and Difference* (1986), and *In the House of Oshugbo: A Collection of Essays on Wole Soyinka* (1988). He published an autobiography in 1994 entitled *Colored People*. His important theoretical/critical book-length studies, which will be examined in detail below, include *Figures in Black: Words, Signs, and the Racial Self* (1987), *The Signifying Monkey: A Theory of African-American Literary Criticism* (1988), and *Loose Canons: Notes on the Culture Wars* (1992).

In a 1991 interview with Jerry W. Ward, Jr., Gates remarks that "like most people who take the study of culture seriously, I distrust boundaries, I distrust border patrols, I don't want to be told that something is 'outside.'"[3] This desire to break down barriers between normally segregated domains, to show that items commonly excluded from a particular field can and should be placed within that field, is the central, underlying theme of Gates's work. Whether his focus is the literary text or larger social/cultural constructs, Gates recognizes the existence, and frequently the necessity, of separate, distinct realms, but at the same time he works to bring them together without obliterating their individual identities. He shares with de Man and other post-structuralists a double vision that sees things as interwoven with and often defined in terms of their opposites. Identity, for Gates, is a relational function, always capable, at least in theory, of being undone and reformulated.

Gates's first book, *Figures in Black,* is a collection of nine essays, several of which originally appeared elsewhere in other forms. As he notes in the acknowledgments section of the book, these essays date as far back as 1979; three are reprinted from Dexter Fisher and Robert B. Stepto's *Afro-American Literature: The Reconstruction of Instruction* (1979). Also included are such noteworthy early texts, revised and with different titles, as "Criticism in the Jungle," first in print in *Black Literature and Literary Theory,* and "On the Blackness of Blackness: A Critique of the Sign and the Signifying Monkey," initially published in 1983 in *Critical Inquiry.*[4] Read in chronological order, these pieces trace the course of Gates's thought as it developed over the first years of his career.

Gates begins his substantial introduction to *Figures in Black* by stating that "I have tried to draw upon the extraordinarily rich and diverse body of contemporary literary theory to analyze the writing of African and Afro-American authors published in English between the eighteenth century and the present" (xv). One of the several achievements of this book is its introduction of black texts with which the average reader is likely not familiar. Many of the works Gates analyzes are not a part of the Western canon—the group of literary texts commonly studied in American and European universities or read by the educated public. He gives lengthy plot summaries, quotes extensively, and closely examines author biographies in an effort to acquaint his readers with these valuable books.

For example, in the fifth chapter, "Parallel Discursive Universes: Fictions of the Self in Harriet E. Wilson's *Our Nig,*" Gates discusses in detail the genesis, the author, the reception (or lack of reception), the plot, and the themes of the nineteenth-century black autobiographical novel, *Our Nig.* His concern to familiarize the reader with the surface facts of this text is especially apparent in the final thirteen pages of the essay where he constructs an elaborate chart in parallel columns, one column outlining the plot and the other relating biographical details from Wilson's life to specific plot elements (150–63). Such detailed factual information is needed because this text, which Gates accidentally discovered in a Manhattan bookstore in May 1981 (125), and its author "seem to have been ignored or overlooked both by her [contemporary] 'colored brethren universally' and by even the most scrupulous scholars during the next hundred and twenty-three years" (128–29). By exposing the reader to this obscure but valuable work, Gates implicitly promotes its future study and thereby moves to extend the Western canon.

As important as his effort is to cross boundaries by presenting previously unknown texts, by bringing into the canon works that have been excluded from it, Gates's primary aim and principal accomplishment in *Figures in Black* is the application of "the extraordinarily rich and diverse body of contemporary literary theory" to these black works. Gates, in the introduction to his book, maintains that the vast majority of scholarship on black literature has focussed on raw content, has treated this literature almost exclusively in sociological or political terms, as if its only value were the messages it conveyed about "the black experience." Very little attention has been paid to form, to style and structure. In an attempt to counter this tendency, Gates determines to highlight "the most repressed element of Afro-American criticism: the language of the text" (xxviii). Without denying the importance or necessity of sociologically oriented criticism, he sets out to treat black works with the same respect that critics have traditionally accorded white works: as literature, as complex structures of metaphors, symbols, personifications, and other literary devices. It is to this end that he evokes contemporary theory, much of which is concerned with the intricate workings of literary language.

As Craig Werner points out, certain African American critics such as Joyce A. Joyce, Norman Harris, and Barbara Christian have criticized Gates for "imposing an inappropriate (continental, academic, Euro-American, abstract) vocabulary on Afro-American materials. . . ."[5] It should be noted, however, that though Gates consciously borrows from such vocabularies, at the same time he works to modify and extend them. The encounter between white theories and black texts must inevitably, he maintains, alter the character and understanding of both. "[W]e must," he asserts, "respect the integrity, the tradition, of the black work of art by bringing to bear upon the explication of its meaning all of the attention to language that we may learn from several developments in contemporary theory" (xx–xxi). But he also points out that "by the very process of application, we re-create, through revision, the critical theory at hand" (xxi). To bring Euro-American theory to bear upon the black text is to translate the text into alien terms, but this act of translation itself alters the theory as the theory is molded to fit the black text. Gates's ultimate goal, which he never fully achieves in *Figures in Black,* is to develop a uniquely African American theory of literary interpretation. "My charged advocacy of the relevance of contemporary theory to reading Afro-American and African literature closely," he announces, "has been designed as the prelude to the definition of principles of literary criticism peculiar to the black literary traditions themselves, related to and compatible with contemporary theory generally, yet 'indelibly black'. . . " (xix). This aim becomes his principal pursuit in his second book, *The Signifying Monkey.*

Gates devotes the first chapter of *Figures in Black,* "Literary Theory and the Black Tradition," to explaining why most early commentary focussed on the extraliterary purposes black texts might serve rather than on their aesthetic merits. In the eighteenth and nineteenth centuries, and even into the twentieth century, there was considerable debate among whites over whether blacks were equally as human as whites, or even whether blacks were human at all. Gates cites comments by an array of notable European and American philosophers who outrightly relegated blacks to an inferior, secondary status. For example, in "Of

HENRY LOUIS GATES, JR.: BLACK STUDIES

National Characters" (1748), David Hume wrote that "'I am apt to suspect the negroes and in general all the other species of men (for there are four or five different kinds) to be naturally inferior to the whites. There never was a civilized nation of any other complexion than white, nor even any individual eminent either in action or speculation'" (18). *Blackness,* for these philosophers, became "a trope of absence," a word signifying a group of people who lacked essential qualities of civilized humanity (21).

For Enlightenment thinkers, the ability to read and write was chief among the qualities that defined the human. Gates notes that "mastery of the arts and letters was Enlightenment Europe's sign of that solid line of division between human being and thing" (25). Consequently, early black literature, in America and abroad, was used by whites opposed to the predominant attitude, espoused by such prominent figures as Hume, to prove that blacks were indeed fully human; that they were not "things" but intelligent beings capable of the same sort of thinking and feeling as whites. This literature "came under scrutiny not primarily literary" (27), but rather was viewed simply as evidence of "the black's potential for 'culture'" (4). Gates examines the work of several early black writers, such as Phillis Wheatley and Ignatius Sancho, noting that fine points of structure and style were generally ignored by these authors' contemporaries, their texts being used more generally by those rejecting prevailing racist sentiments to establish "the African's potential to *deserve* inclusion in the human community" (9).

The impulse to assert the humanity of blacks, to show that they were as capable of literacy as were whites, was obviously noble and necessary. This enterprise constituted a crucial stage in the development of African American culture. The unfortunate consequence of this attitude, however, was to firmly ensconce a strictly sociological, use-value orientation toward black writing that persisted into the 1970s. In the 1920s, Gates points out, "the [black] critic became social reformer, and literature became an instrument for the social and ethical betterment of the black person" (30). And in the 1940s, 1950s, and 1960s, with Ralph Ellison, James Baldwin, and Imamu Baraka, "message reigned supreme; form became a mere convenience or, worse, a contrivance" (31). Says Gates, "black critics forgot that writers approached things through words, not the other way around" (30).

The remaining essays in *Figures in Black* are divided into two sections, "The Literature of the Slave" and "Black Structures of Feeling." The first of the two essays on Frederick Douglass in the first section is an especially good illustration of Gates's early attempts to bring contemporary white theory and critical terminology to bear upon black texts, to correct the historical legacy of ignoring black literary language and form. Gates opens "Binary Oppositions in Chapter One of *Narrative of the Life of Frederick Douglass an American Slave Written by Himself*" by establishing and defining the slave narrative as a distinct literary genre. "[N]arratives of the escaped slave became during the three decades before the Civil War, the most popular form of written discourse in the country" (81), he begins. He proceeds to delineate this literary type's general characteristics, drawing upon European and American forms. "The slave narrative," Gates theorizes, "is a countergenre, a mediation between the novel of sentiment and the picaresque, oscillating somewhere between the two in a bipolar moment, set in motion by the mode of the

HENRY LOUIS GATES, JR.: BLACK STUDIES

confession" (81). After carefully explaining his terms, he positions Douglass's *Narrative* of 1845 squarely in the slave narrative tradition, calling it a text "that exploited the potential [of the genre] and came to determine the shape of language in the slave narrative" (83).

Having firmly situated Douglass's *Narrative* on formal literary terrain, in the second portion of the essay Gates evokes the structuralist notion of binary opposition to further explicate the machinery of Douglass's text. "When any two terms are set in opposition to each other," he explains, drawing on the work of Roman Jakobson, Morris Halle, Claude Levi-Strauss, and Fredric Jameson, all white critics in the structuralist camp, "the reader is forced to explore qualitative similarities and differences, to make some connection, and, therefore, to derive some meaning from points of disjunction" (88). Central to the structuralist concept of meaning is the idea that individual items make sense not in isolation but in relation to each other. Binary oppositions pair two distinct items, creating sense and significance for each through each's similarities with and differences from the other. Gates shows how Douglass's text utilizes such oppositions in order to make its points. He cites a passage in which Douglass compares his and other slaves' lives to those of animals and to natural cycles: "By far the larger part of the slaves know as little of their ages as horses know of theirs, and it is the wish of most masters within my knowledge to keep their slaves thus ignorant. I do not remember to have ever met a slave who could tell of his birthday, they seldom come nearer to it than planting-time, harvest-time, cherry-time, spring-time, or fall-time" (88).

Gates analyzes this text, in structuralist fashion, by arguing that Douglass's juxtapositions of opposites, his yoking of slaves and animals, blacks and nature, show up the barbarity of the slave-owning system. The system perpetuates a perverse mentality which dehumanizes blacks, equating them with the nonhuman world (89–90). The reader "derive[s] some meaning from points of disjunction" in the juxtapositions in that he or she understands just how forced they are; knows that despite what the plantation owners encourage to the contrary, slaves are radically other than livestock and natural processes. As Gates puts it, the linking of blacks with the nonhuman world "suggests overwhelmingly the completely arbitrary relationship between description and meaning. . . " (89). Just because slaves are defined by their owners as subhuman does not mean that they are subhuman; there is another, more humane and enlightened way to constitute black identity, and Douglass's binary oppositions implicitly call for this new definition.

In the course of the final eight pages of the essay, Gates deftly details other specific, subtle ways in which Douglass's text exploits binary oppositions, noting that it does so throughout in order to show that the plantation owner's code "stands in defiance of natural and moral order" (92). Contemporary theory—in this case structuralism—becomes a tool for deciphering a black text. The text's meaning is illuminated by the white theoretical construct, while the theory is tailored to serve the black end of critiquing racism. Formal analysis crosses over into political commentary; a structural device—binary opposition—implicitly damns the plantation system and urges its abolition.

The second section of *Figures in Black* opens with an essay, "Dis and Dat: Dialect and the Descent," which like "Binary

Oppositions" relies upon contemporary theory, though less exclusively than does the Douglass piece. Here Gates links an African cultural practice, the use of ceremonial masks to convey coded messages, with certain Euro-American theories of language, which view words as simultaneously conveying and hiding meaning. He thereby suggests a general model for interpreting literary texts as systems of signs that function like masks, the text's deep senses being disguised by and implied in what it explicitly, outwardly says (168–83). Such a model, Gates contends, is particularly useful for interpreting a specific form of black literature: that written in black dialect. One of the several examples of dialect that Gates cites is from an old Negro spiritual: "'Gwine to sit down at the welcome table / Gwine to feast off milk and honey.'" These verses, he explains, are a translation of verses from a standard European hymn: "'At this table we'll sit down,/ Christ will gird himself and serve us sweet manna all around'" (190). One of the words Gates focuses upon is "'Gwine,'" a term "still commonly found in black speech." The "full import" of this word, he argues, "goes far beyond its referent, 'I am going to,' and implies far more" (191). Part of the "far more" it implies is "the completion, the restoration of harmony in what had heretofore been a universe out of step somehow" (191). The term, in the sound and sense, suggests movement toward an afterlife in which the slave will be removed from his present alienated and discordant condition and restored to his rightful, blessed estate as fully integrated in "the bosom of God" (191). The implicit meaning of "Gwine" hides behind and is expressed through its explicit, surface sense—"I am going to." "Gwine," like the other words in the spiritual, is "coded, danced speech" (186), a mask that simultaneously disguises and conveys a store of uniquely black thoughts and feelings.

"Dis and Dat" comes closer than "Binary Oppositions" to achieving the goal, announced in the introduction, of devising a "literary criticism peculiar to the black literary traditions themselves, related to and compatible with contemporary theory generally, yet 'indelibly black.'. . ." The former essay, unlike the latter, concentrates on a distinctly black form of language and uses a black conceptual model, in addition to white theory, to interpret this language. Coming closer still to this goal is the final essay in *Figures in Black,* "The 'Blackness of Blackness': A Critique of the Sign and the Signifying Monkey." Here Gates introduces, without fully developing, an "'indelibly black'" figure for interpretation, the signifying monkey. This figure, elaborated, amplified, and extensively applied, becomes the focus of Gates's second book.

The Signifying Monkey, which won the 1989 American Book Award, was praised by John Wideman in the *New York Times Book Review* as "exciting, convincing, provocative, challenging. . . . a generous, long-awaited gift."[6] Observed T. O. Mason, *"The Signifying Monkey* will be one of the central theoretical and critical texts for a number of years. . . ."[7] The book is divided into two sections, "A Theory of the Tradition" and "Reading the Tradition." In the three chapters in the first section, Gates explores the roots of and fully defines a black interpretive theory grounded in the figure of the signifying monkey. In the four chapters in the second section he applies this theory to detailed readings of specific black texts.

The book's opening chapter, "A Myth of Origins: Esu-

Elegbara and the Signifying Monkey," traces African American principles of reading back to native African tales and conceptual models. The mythological trickster Esu-Elegbara is, according to Gates, the ultimate figure for the African notion of interpretation. This character, which has its source in "the Fon and Yoruba cultures of Benin and Nigeria," assumes different names and guises in different cultures.[8] He "is called Esu-Elegbara in Nigeria and Legba among the Fon in Benin. His New World figurations include Exú in Brazil, Echu-Elegua in Cuba, Papa Legba . . . in the pantheon of the loa of Vaudou of Haiti, and Papa La Bas in the loa of Hoodoo in the United States" (5). The Signifying Monkey, which Gates examines in detail in later chapters, is the "functional equivalent" of Esu-Elegbara (11). In all his incarnations, Gates summarizes, Esu "is the indigenous black metaphor for the literary critic" and represents "the study of methodological principles of interpretation itself, or what the literary critic does" (9).

The fundamental methodological principle that the critic relies upon is indeterminacy. Esu stands for the inexhaustible quality of interpretation, for the fact that texts do not have fixed and single meanings but are instead subject to multiple readings. Esu, in Gates's words, is the "Yoruba figure of indeterminacy itself" (11). He is "a metaphor for the uncertainties of explication, for the open-endedness of every literary text" (21). This sense of indeterminacy is perhaps best illustrated in the Esu myth called "The Two Friends." In this tale, Esu tests the bond between two longtime companions by donning a cloth cap, the right side of which is black and the left side white, and riding his horse down a path between them as they work in adjacent fields. When the friends compare what they have seen after Esu passes by, one insists that the cap the rider was wearing is black and the other that it is white. Their disagreement escalates into a full-scale fight, which the neighbors eventually have to break up. Esu returns to the scene, sees the commotion, and asks the pair to explain the problem. After hearing their stories, he reveals the secret of his hat, informing them that both their reports of what they saw are correct (32–34). He further admonishes them to take note "'that he who does not put Esu first in all his doings has himself to blame if things misfire'" (35). "The folly depicted here," Gates interprets, "is to insist—to the point of rupture of the always fragile bond of a human institution—on one determinant meaning, itself determined by vantage point and the mode one employs to see" (35). The moral of this tale is much the same as the moral of the tale Paul de Man tells: a single text can have contradictory meanings that oppose and deny each other, yet are intimately connected and equally valid.

African-based folklore, then, like Western post-structuralist theories, sees the informed reader as one who manipulates and plays with tricky, bottomless texts. He or she is an Esu who understands the contradictory complexities of interpretation. In the African American tradition, this reader is personified in the figure of the Signifying Monkey. The Monkey first appeared in tales which "seem to have had their origins in slavery." Since the beginning of this century, Gates notes, "hundreds of these [tales] have been recorded. . ." (51). The second and third chapters of *The Signifying Monkey* are devoted to analyzing and illustrating the linguistic practice—Signifyin(g)—that the Monkey represents, a practice, Gates maintains, that is central to African

American concepts of reading, writing, and speech.

Signifyin(g), a distinctly black word which is capitalized and ends in " yin(g)" rather than " ying" in order to distinguish it from the white " signifying," is a form of revision, a game of difference that one text plays in relation to another. A text is Signifyin(g) when it retains the basic terms of some source text but rewrites them in a radically new way. As James Olney explains, Signifyin(g) is " a responsive going-beyond in the same language."[9] It is, in Gates's words, " black double-voicedness . . . [that] always entails formal revision and intertextual relation. . . . Repetition, with a signal difference, is fundamental to the nature of Signifyin(g). . ." (51). The black Signifyin(g) author capitalizes upon the open-endedness of texts, demonstrating new directions in which a work may be taken when read from a fresh perspective. Like Esu, the Signifyin(g) author understands that a text seen as white can also be seen as black; he or she realizes that a work may be so dramatically altered through reinterpretation that it expresses a meaning opposite to the one originally ascribed to it.

Perhaps the best examples of Signifyin(g) are to be found not in literature but in music. The improvisational revisions that jazz executes in relation to standard musical scores epitomize the act of Signifyin(g). For instance, a typical exercise for the black jazz musician is to redo some well-known white tune, embellishing and varying it to create a distinctive new sound. Gates gives as an example John Coltrane's rendition of Julie Andrews's "My Favorite Things." Coltrane's interpretation of Andrews's song voices directions implicit in it—this is the way Andrews *might* have sounded —that she herself does not develop. He " repeats" her text in radically different terms, creating in the process an highly original piece of music. This musical repetition with a difference serves as a useful and illuminating analogy for verbal Signifyin(g) (63–64, 104).

A simple example of verbal Signifyin(g) can be found in the third chapter of *The Signifying Monkey*. Gates here cites a poem chanted by black children while skipping rope. Apparently created in East Texas sometime after the forced integration of public schools in the late 1950s, this rhyme plays off of a white racist text. The white text reads "Two, four, six, eight/We ain't gonna integrate." The black, Signifyin(g) text also includes these lines but adds to them "Eight, six, four, two,/Bet you sons-of-bitches do" (103). Gates observes that this is an instance of "rhetorical naming by indirection" (103). The black poem makes a not-so-veiled reference to laws passed about this time which negate the racist wish expressed in the white jingle. The revised text functions as a form of parody or pastiche, both common modes of Signifyin(g), by repeating a precursor narrative but adding to it a difference that subverts the intent of the original (103). The black text, that is, discloses an implicit, dormant direction buried in the white text; the white words are not the end of the story but can be elaborated upon, stylized in black, to reverse their intention.

The second section of *The Signifying Monkey,* "Reading the Tradition," consists of extensive applications of Signifyin(g) to the analysis of the black literary canon. Perhaps the most interesting and representative of these four essays is the first, "The Trope of the Talking Book." Here Gates identifies a figurative device—a book that can speak—which frequently appears in black narra-

HENRY LOUIS GATES, JR.: BLACK STUDIES

tives. He traces the history of its use, showing how over the years African American authors have borrowed this device from each other, revising it in the process to create fresh meanings.

According to Gates, the Talking Book first appears in James Albert Ukawsaw Gronniosaw's *A Narrative of the Most Remarkable Particulars in the Life of Albert Ukawsaw Gronniosay, An African Prince, As Related by Himself,* published in the 1770s (132). In the course of this lengthy autobiography, Gronniosaw tells about being taken by slave traders from his native Africa to Europe. One day, while aboard the ship, he observed with great surprise his master's prayer book talk as the master read to the ship's crew. Wishing to have the book speak to him personally, Gronniosaw followed his master to the place where he put this text down. When no one was looking, he picked it up and placed it to his ear, hoping it would say something to him. Greatly disappointed when it does not, Gronniosaw concluded that "'every body and every thing despised me because I was black'" (136).

Gates interprets this story of the Talking Book as "renam[ing] the received tradition in European letters that the mask of blackness worn by Gronniosaw and his countrymen was a trope of absence" (136–37). With respect to Western, "civilized" discourse, the African, illiterate Gronniosaw does not exist. Since the language of the book is not the language of the slave, the white master's text does not, cannot, acknowledge this black man's presence by speaking to him. Gronniosaw discovers that he must be integrated into European modes of thought, symbolized by the book and the ability to read and write that it represents, in order to be accepted as a fully human being in the white man's world. Thus, "some forty-five years later [after this incident] Gronniosaw writes a text [*A Narrative*] that speaks his face into existence among the authors and texts of the Western tradition" (137–38). He establishes a human presence, as defined by white culture, by making a book talk; the text he writes vocalizes his thoughts and feelings. He thus overcomes the painful lack he earlier felt in his experience with his master's prayer book.

A second important text in which the Talking Book appears is John Marrant's *The Narrative of the Lord's Wonderful Dealings with John Marrant, A Black.* Marrant, born in New York in 1755, was actually not a slave but rather the son of free black parents. Following a deep religious conversion that alienated him from his family, he wandered into the wilderness near his South Carolina home and was there captured by Indians. As Marrant relates his tale in *The Narrative,* he was eventually taken before the Cherokee king, at which point the king's daughter, who was also in attendance, became fascinated by the Bible he carried. Marrant complies with the king's request that he read from this book, and following the reading, the mesmerized daughter snatches the volume from Marrant's hands. She is greatly agitated when she discovers that this text will not speak to her. It speaks, she believes, to Marrant, and she cannot understand why it will not do her the same honor (142–43).

What Marrant has done here, Gates argues, is subvert Gronniosaw's equation between blackness and absence. In Gronniosaw the text will not speak to the black man. In Marrant a black man is the one to whom the text *will* speak. As Gates puts it, whereas in Gronniosaw's version of the Talking Book trope "voice presupposes a white or assimilated face," in Marrant's revision of this figure "voice presupposes . . . a black face" (144). Marrant is in the same position in relation to his Indian captors as the white masters are in relation to Gronniosaw: equipped to show up the nonpresence and nonidentity of an illiterate, non-Christian, and therefore "savage" race.

In both texts the Talking Book is a device for distinguishing between the literate and the illiterate, the fully human and the nonhuman. Marrant's difference from Gronniosaw lies in his use of this device to demonstrate that the black man is capable of possessing from the outset the literacy, and consequent fully human status, that in Gronniosaw he must work to acquire. Marrant's narrative, in short, is Signifyin(g) upon Gronniosaw's. Marrant borrows from Gronniosaw a central figure, the Talking Book, but recontextualizes and refashions it in such a way as to make a point that differs radically from his predecessor's. In Gates's words, Marrant "seeks to reverse the received trope by displacement and substitution. All the key terms of Gronniosaw's trope are present in Marrant's revision, but the 'original' pattern has been rearranged significantly" (145). Marrant capitalizes upon the indeterminacy, the open-endedness, of the Talking Book trope. This figure, he demonstrates, is not restricted to implying that black people must earn the status of civilized, educated human beings and are therefore innately inferior to whites; it can also be used to affirm that African Americans, like whites, have this status to begin with and are thus in a position of superiority in relation to other races which are uncivilized and uneducated (144–46).

In the remainder of the essay, Gates closely examines three other black texts, each of which further revises the Talking Book.

He details Signifyin(g) relationships, highlighting swerves that one work executes in relation to another and noting the implications of these swerves for the development of the black canon. The originality of each of the three works, Gates emphasizes, is to be measured not by the degree to which it is a creation of something from nothing, but instead to the extent that its author imaginatively manipulates the Talking Book trope as employed by a forerunner. Signifyin(g) generates new meaning—new and original literary works—through subversive boundary crossings, revealing that every text contains hidden within it the seeds of some other, radically different text. It is the successive, chronological progression of such crossings through history that constitutes and propagates the black literary tradition.

In all his discussions of Signifyin(g), Gates sounds very much like a prominent white theorist who was teaching at Yale when Gates was a student, Harold Bloom. As noted in the introduction to this book, Bloom argues that literature is produced through anxiety-driven revisionary strife between authors; by one text's creative swerves from another. This view is so close to Gates's that Kenneth Warren has claimed "one can read *The Signifying Monkey* as Gates's rewriting of Bloom's oedipal drama for the black tradition in which psychology gives way, once again, to rhetoric and 'Signifyin(g)' replaces "'anxiety.'"[10] Though Gates contends that the notion of Signifyin(g) is built into the black tradition, that he is identifying a practice inherent in black texts, one might legitimately ask whether or not he would have "discovered" this practice in the first place, or at least whether or not he would have articulated it in the terms he does, if he had not already been familiar with Bloom's influential theory.

Gates's next book, *Loose Canons: Notes on the Culture Wars,* is a collection of ten essays, all but two of which were originally published elsewhere, the earliest in 1985. As the title suggests, this study is concerned primarily with political and social issues, though certainly the analysis of particular literary works comes into play. The aim of these pieces, as Gates states it in the introduction, is to promote recognition of contemporary American society as "profoundly fissured by nationality, ethnicity, race, class, and gender" but at the same time to encourage transcendence of those divisions through a perspective that "respects both differences and commonalities . . . that seeks to comprehend the diversity of human culture."[11] The answer to social strife, Gates believes, lies not in single-toned homogenization, but instead in communication and intermixing across boundaries, in valuing the uniqueness of different cultural formations yet being willing to construct new, multitextured, hybrid realities. He champions a "pluralism" which "sees culture as porous, dynamic, and interactive, rather than as the fixed property of particular ethnic groups" (xvi). In making these points, Gates frequently echoes, sometimes in almost identical language, points he has made in his first two books. This is not surprising since several of these pieces were originally written prior to the publication of *Figures in Black* and *The Signifying Monkey.*

The book is divided into three sections, "Literature," "The Profession," and "Society." He begins the final chapter of the first section, "Talking Black: Critical Signs of the Times," by citing Alexander Crummell, a nineteenth-century black intellectual who sought to establish his equality with whites by mastering their culture. Crummell, who received a degree from Cambridge, demonstrated through his education and writings that a black man could use the English language as proficiently and be as well versed in the literary canon of the West as any white man (72–75). Gates expresses his admiration for Crummell, referring to his efforts as "pioneering" and labeling him "the intellectual godfather of W. E. B. DuBois" (72). He also notes the positive model that Crummell and others like him established for contemporary African American thinkers. "Learning the master's tongue," Gates observes, "for our generation of critics, has been an act of empowerment, whether that tongue be New Criticism, humanism, structuralism, Marxism, poststructuralism, feminism, new historicism, or any other 'ism'" (75).

Gates maintains, however, that it is time for a change of tactics. It is time for blacks to move out of strictly imitative, mimicking modes of thought and into more original, distinctly black forms. Gates focuses his remarks about the study of literature, but this study is, he points out, necessarily political and has ramifications for the larger black cultural condition; to develop African American literary scholarship is to advance the status of African Americans in American society as a whole.

One of Gates's chief recommendations is what he has preached and practiced since his first book: the constitution of a black theory of literary criticism by Signifyin(g) upon white theory; discovering critical principles in black texts themselves and refashioning white practices to serve black ends. "This is the challenge of the critic of black literature in the 1980s," Gates asserts in words almost identical to ones he used in the introduction to *Figures in Black,* "not to shy away from white power—

that is literary theory—but to translate it into the black idiom, *renaming* principles of criticism where appropriate, but especially *naming* indigenous black principles of criticism and applying them to our own texts" (79).

The redefinition of what it means to be black through the promotion of black forms of thought that do not merely repeat the lessons of white culture is possible, Gates believes, because race is not an essence but rather a malleable social construct (79). That is, he rejects the idea that there is an innate, God-ordained black way of thinking and being. All racial identities, beyond skin pigmentation, are made by people, not prescribed by nature. They thus can be refashioned and resituated at will. Gates explicitly reveals his desire to integrate, rather than segregate, black, white, and other cultural identities when he writes: "My task, as I see it, is to help guarantee that black and so-called Third World literature is taught to black and Third World and white students by black and Third World and white professors in heretofore white mainstream departments of literature . . . " (80). Black literature and literary theory, and the larger social forms they imply, are envisioned by Gates as complementary to and impinging upon white culture, as equalizing correctives in a monochromatically white world. Thus, the reviewer of *Loose Canons* in *The Economist* who wrote that Gates is making a case for "black cultural nationalism" which, finally, "reimpose[s] segregation in higher education"[12] misses the point. James D. Bloom in the *New York Times Book Review* comes much closer to understanding Gates when he observes that "the author [Gates] argues that knowing African American literature is essential for all Americans because black voices are central in shaping the national culture."[13]

In the second essay, "Integrating the American Mind," of the second section of *Loose Canons,* Gates extends and emphasizes the argument that to recognize the existence of distinct cultural formations is not to opt for their segregation. In fact, he lobbies here for a reformed system of education that would involve embracing and cross-fertilizing multiple cultural perspectives. American universities, he contends, must break away from the status quo course of mining only the glories of "the best that has been thought by white males in Greco-Roman, Judeo-Christian traditions" (113). They need to provide an education that also "account[s] for the comparable eloquence of the African, Asian, the Latin American, and the Middle Eastern traditions" (113). Studying white Western literature and philosophy in concert with that from other national and ethnic traditions, he believes, can only be "mutually enriching" (114). It can help eliminate the "divisive us/them" mentality (116) and contribute to "expand[ing] the constricted boundaries of human sympathy, of social tolerance" (117).

The tone of this essay is not angry. Gates does not feel that lingering white cultural chauvinism, and the racism it spawns, is the result of a "white conspiracy." Despite ensconced curriculums that disproportionately favor white culture and thought over black, he believes that there is a genuine impulse in most universities to change things: "in general, our colleges really are devoted to [achieving] diversity: people are genuinely upset when they fail to incorporate diversity among their students and faculty" (107). Gates is optimistic. He is convinced that, in spite of its opponents in society at large, multiculturalism can flourish. "I believe we can rethink the role of a liberal education without

HENRY LOUIS GATES, JR.: BLACK STUDIES

the conceptual residue of cultural nationalism," he writes, because "many scholars have already begun to do so" (112). "Integrating the American Mind" identifies some very real racial problems in our society, but it hopefully pushes for a program of boundary crossings between the white and black worlds which, Gates thinks, can be, and to a limited degree already have been, achieved.

Though he refuses to adopt a resentful, victimized attitude, Gates is obviously bothered by and objects to the presence of racism in America. In "What's in a Name? Some Meanings of Blackness," the first essay of the third section of *Loose Canons,* he relates several incidents of prejudice that he has experienced over the years and registers his profound and justifiable displeasure with them (131–36). But because he believes that race and attitudes toward it are made things and not fixed essences, he thinks that it is possible for American society to change directions. Through education and the labor of a new breed of black, and white, scholars, Gates hopes that our society can alter the racist realities it has created and thereby alleviate, if not altogether eliminate, the problem of prejudice.

He finds encouraging signs of change in contemporary African American authors such as Toni Morrison. The goal of these black writers "seems to be to create a fiction *beyond* the color line, one that takes the blackness of the culture for granted, as a springboard to write about those human emotions that we [blacks] share with everyone else. . . " (147). Gates here repeats his desire to integrate rather than segregate. But even though he urges commonality, he also recognizes, in this essay as in the others in *Loose Canons,* obvious differences between white and black cultural heritages. Gates denounces the myth that black society has been separate from, and made no contributions to, white society; but at the same time he acknowledges that the two worlds have been, and continue to be, distinct. "The idea that African-American culture is exclusively a thing apart, separate from the whole, having no influence on the shape and shaping of American culture, is a racialist fiction" (151). His point is that white scholars have failed to acknowledge the important role black culture has played in creating the dominant white culture; it is not to rewrite history so as to suggest that the two cultures have been, in actuality, so thoroughly integrated that they constitue a seamless identity.

In none of his books and essays does Gates wish, implicitly or explicitly, for the African American heritage to somehow cancel Western, white civilization; he has no desire to replace the treasures of the white world with those of the black. What he wants is for black culture to be an equal voice in a multicultural conversation, a voice that might grow and develop, overlapping with and diverging from, but always in some way coloring, the white voices. This is the impulse motivating all of Gates's work, from *Figures in Black,* to *The Signifying Monkey,* through *Loose Canons.* His aim has been to promote black literature and literary criticism so that it might achieve the same respect and exert the same cultural influence that white literature and theory always have.

CHAPTER FOUR

Elaine Showalter
Feminism

Elaine Showalter was born in 1941 in Cambridge, Massachusetts.[1] She attended Bryn Mawr from 1958 to 1962, a period to which she refers in a 1986 interview as "the nadir of women's education in this country."[2] Upon graduation, she entered the M.A. program at Brandeis University, where she completed her degree in 1964.[3] In 1970, she received her Ph.D. from the University of California, Davis. Showalter taught English at Rutgers University and from there went to Princeton, where she is currently Professor of English.[4] Among the many collections of essays she has edited and contributed to are *The New Feminist Criticism: Essays on Women, Literature, and Theory* (1984) and *Daughters of Decadence: Women Writers at the Fin de siècle* (1993). To date, she has written four books, *A Literature of Their Own: Women Writers from Charlotte Bronte to Doris Lessing* (1977), *The Female Malady: Women, Madness and English Culture, 1830–1980* (1985), *Sexual Anarchy: Gender and Culture at the Fin de siècle* (1990), and *Sister's Choice: Tradition and Change in American Women's Writing* (1991).

In one of her best-known essays, "Feminist Criticism in the Wilderness," originally published in *Critical Inquiry* in 1981, Showalter champions "a feminist criticism that is genuinely woman centered."[5] Such projects she labels "gynocriticism," noting that their focus should be "the history, styles, themes, genres, and structures of writing by women; the psychodynamics of female creativity; the trajectory of the individual or collective female career; and the evolution and laws of a female literary tradition."[6] There are, Showalter maintains, four principal divisions of gynocentric theory: biological, linguistic, psychoanalytic, and cultural.[7] She counts herself in the cultural camp, declaring that "a theory based on a model of women's culture can provide . . . a more complete and satisfying way to talk about the specificity and difference of women's writing than theories based in biology, linguistics, or psychoanalysis."[8] She prefers to understand women's literature in terms of the social and historical forces which produce it rather than as the expression of an innate feminine nature, the workings of isolated female psyches, or the product of laws of female language usage. Though Showalter's announced goal is to define and investigate women's culture, she is acutely aware of the impossibility of completely separating female forms of expression from larger social structures. "[N]o publication," she writes, "is fully independent from the economic and political pressures of the male-dominated society."[9]

The general concerns and emphases of this essay echo throughout the body of Showalter's work. Her focus has certainly always been the feminine, both inside and outside of literature; she has consistently attempted to identify and describe that which constitutes woman. Her books and essays, however, stress the point she makes in "Feminist Criticism in the Wilderness": though the category of woman can be isolated for analysis, it nonetheless interconnects with a host of other domains—masculinity, class, race, etc.—and cannot be fully understood apart from them. Gender, Showalter repeatedly argues in keeping with the culturally oriented stance she takes in the *Critical Inquiry* piece, is a social construct, not an eternal, pre-given, natural essence. All her claims are ultimately grounded in the assumption that male and female identities, excluding anatomical traits, are fabricated by communities of people, not genetically programmed into the individual.

Showalter's general strategy is to divide feminine experience and expression into phases or types, each phase or type conceived of as the product of a particular culture at a particular time. Her view of the feminine as a social product allows her to posit change and development in the roles and conceptions of women through space and time and, more important, it enables her to postulate improved models of femininity for the future. Showalter is no mere recorder of female history and trends; rather, she evaluates as she describes, suggesting problems with current and past scenarios and projecting an improved tomorrow.

Showalter's first book, *A Literature of Their Own,* was written in 1972–73 but not published until January 1977.[10] A groundbreaking text, this examination of English women novelists represents, as Showalter declares, "the first book of feminist criticism published by any major university press."[11] Critics generally greeted it with high praise. In a July 1977 review in *Encounter,* Rosemary Jackson called *A Literature of Their Own* "quite simply, the best study of women's fiction to date." It is "original, suggestive, thoroughly documented, and richly detailed," she declared, a text "scholarly without being abstract or abstruse."[12]

In the opening chapter, Showalter clearly states her purpose:

"This book is an effort to describe the female literary tradition in the English novel from the generation of the Brontës to the present day, and to show how the development of this tradition is similar to the development of any literary subculture."[13] She firmly believes that there are qualities in women's writing that distinguish it from men's, that it is meaningful and useful to speak of a female literature which, while part of a larger whole, has an identity separate from that of the male tradition. Women's writing, furthermore, constitutes a "literary subculture" in that it is produced and defined through conflicts and collusions with culturally dominant masculine views and values (11).

Showalter notes that though it is impossible to say exactly when women in England began writing fiction, it is possible to determine that "almost no sense of communality and self-awareness is apparent among women writers [in England] before the 1840s..." (18). It is at this point that the female literary subculture she intends to study begins to take shape. This subculture extends and develops, she demonstrates through the course of her book, from that moment to the present.

Showalter divides the female British literary tradition into three phases: the Feminine, 1840–80; the Feminist, 1880–1920; and the Female, 1920–present (13). Cautioning that these demarcations are only approximate and that the phases sometimes overlap—particular writers may demonstrate characteristics of more than one of the three stages—Showalter proceeds to equate each period with what she perceives to be a particular stage of development in the history of subcultures in general. Thus, the Feminine phase is one of "*imitation* of the prevailing modes of the dominant tradition, and *internalization* of its standards of art and its views on social roles"; the Feminist phase constitutes a "*protest* against those standards and values [of the dominant culture], and *advocacy* of minority rights and values, including a demand for autonomy"; and the Female phase involves "*self-discovery,* a turning inward freed from some of the dependency of opposition, a search for identity" (13). Though each stage represents certain advances over its predecessor, this scheme is not meant to outline a tidy, clear-cut movement from a least satisfactory to a most satisfactory moment in female literary history. Showalter finds flaws in the image of Woman in the third, second, and first stages alike. "I was working in *A Literature of Their Own,*" she remarks in an interview, "against a certain teleological sentimentality . . . [against] the idea of progress, that in every generation women's writing became aesthetically better, politically firmer, linguistically more complicated, morally more challenging, and of course, always more feminist."[14]

Underlying Showalter's notion of phases is one of those central premises found in the *Critical Inquiry* piece that she repeats throughout her books and essays: woman is a socially and historically constructed category, not a fixed identity ordained by nature. Each phase in her history represents a particular form of female literary expression created by cultural forces in play at a specific time. She stresses that in her "investigation of the English novel, I am intentionally looking, not at an innate sexual attitude, but at the ways in which the self-awareness of the woman writer has translated itself into a literary form in a specific place and time-span, how this self-awareness has changed and developed, and where it might lead" (12). There is no attempt to determine how far from or how close to the essential nature of woman each phase falls, since Showalter does not believe in fixed and eternal essences. Both her criticisms and endorsements of the past, as well as her suggestions for the future, are made with respect to her own culturally determined image of the optimum feminine condition.

Following the introductory chapter, Showalter, in the remainder of her book, develops and illustrates in detail each of the three phases of woman's literature. In "Feminine Heroines: Charlotte Brontë and George Eliot," she discusses two principal attitudes that were dominant in the Feminine phase. One of these attitudes is represented in the work of Jane Austen and George Eliot, while the other is epitomized in the texts of George Sand— a French author—and her British inheritor, Charlotte Brontë. Characterizing the Austen-Eliot line is a stance of passivity and restraint; heroines in these two women's novels are emotionally repressed and easily acquiesce to the roles defined for them by society. The Sand-Brontë strain, on the other hand, includes a measure of passion and rebellion; the heroines immerse themselves in "the turbulence of womanly suffering" and refuse wholly and immediately to accept their socially assigned places (102–5). Despite these differences, both lines are united by that quality that Showalter, in the introduction, associates with the Feminine phase: a general, ultimate imitation and internalization of society's dominant male values.

Showalter uses Eliot's *The Mill on the Floss* to illustrate the tendencies of the Austen-Eliot line. Maggie Tulliver, the book's female protagonist, is "the heroine of renunciation" (112). In accord with the age's conception of the female character, she is extremely weak, "self- doubting and unassertive" (127). Her sense of self-esteem is unhealthily tied to the love and approval she receives from a strong, willful man, her brother Tom; Maggie "will sacrifice any legitimate claim of her own personality to avoid rejection by him" (127). Showalter points out that in the majority of the conflicts she endures, Maggie "cannot face the truth about her own feelings and has to persuade herself that other people are making her do things" (128). For example, she ends an unhappy relationship with Philip Wakem not by confronting him with her misgivings, but rather by allowing their secret meetings to be discovered by Tom, who steps in and terminates the association (128). Summing up Tulliver's legacy, Showalter writes: "Maggie is the progenitor of a heroine who identifies passivity and renunciation with womanhood, who finds it easier, more natural, and in a mystical way more satisfying, to destroy herself than to live in a world without opium or fantasy, where she must fight to survive" (131). In these judgments and others, Showalter is, clearly, not simply analyzing the plot of a novel; she is also criticizing a particular mindset, a specific form of feminine consciousness fostered by a specific societal context. She is implicitly pointing out ways of thinking and behaving that contemporary women should avoid and gesturing toward alternative courses they should take in the present.

Brontë's Jane Eyre, the character Showalter cites to illustrate the Sand-Brontë strand of the Feminine phase, is a considerably stronger and more self-directed woman than Maggie Tulliver, though she also finally submits to certain crippling norms of feminine behavior. While at Lowood school, young Jane undergoes instruction in the roles she will be expected to play as a woman. In this convent-like institution to which she is sent by her aunt, she experiences "a prolonged sensual discipline," and is taught to diminish and repress her sexual desires (117). Jane, however, "resists the force of spiritual institutionalization," her rebellion symbolized by the death in her arms of Helen Burns, Lowood's star pupil who has wholly internalized the school's repressive values (118).

Nonetheless, it later becomes evident, in Jane's stint as governess at Thornfield Hall, that the stultifying teachings of Lowood have left residual scars. Confined to an upper floor in Thornfield is Bertha Mason, a woman who in her insanity represents "the incarnation of the flesh, of female sexuality in its most irredeemably bestial and terrifying form" (118). Brontë indirectly associates Jane's sexuality with Bertha's animal madness through Jane's love for Rochester, Bertha's husband. It is only after Bertha dies that Jane will accept Rochester, whose advances she has earlier refused. Read symbolically, this belated acceptance signifies that "the purging of the lusts of the flesh must precede any successful union between Rochester and Jane" (122). Brontë makes it clear, according to Showalter, that Jane's primal sexual self, symbolized by Bertha, must die before she can be joined with this man. When they finally marry, Showalter notes, their union is one of equals because by this point Rochester "has learned how it feels to be helpless and how to accept help," while Jane, "in destroying the dark passion of her own psyche, has become truly her 'own mistress'" (122).

Jane, unlike Maggie, takes control of her life. She will have Rochester not on his terms but on her own. Jane, unlike Maggie, is not totally helpless and passive. Maggie would surely have easily and wholly succumbed to the Lowood system whereas Jane rebels against it. Nonetheless, Jane, like Maggie, is ultimately thwarted in the full expression of herself. The novel finally endorses Lowood's skewed notions of female sexuality. Brontë's equation of female sexual desire with bestial insanity reproduces the school's, and the nineteenth century's, perverse value scheme. The fact that Jane must rid herself of her "crazy" feelings before she can have a "healthy" marriage is, Showalter implies, a sign of her entrapment in the age's perverse, masculine-driven system of values. It is true that Jane's marriage represents "a union of equals," but, as Showalter points out, "in feminine fiction [such as *Jane Eyre*] men and women become equals by submitting to mutual limitation, not by allowing each other mutual growth" (124).

Showalter effectively demonstrates that even in the passionate, rebellious line of Feminine phase fiction there is still a great deal of what she calls in the introduction "*imitation* of the prevailing modes of the dominant tradition, and *internalization* of its standards of art and its views on social roles." She again implicitly criticizes a particular form of female consciousness, condemning the cultural mindset that produced it.

The middle chapters of *A Literature of Their Own* are devoted to a discussion of the second, Feminist phase. Here Showalter examines the works of such writers as Elizabeth Robins and Olive Schreiner, pointing out ways in which these texts directly rebel against masculine standards. This period is the one Showalter considers the least artistically successful. She maintains, as Rosemary Jackson notes, that "its narrow focus on sexual and sexist content seemed to work against a successfully realized novel."[15] The vehemence and didacticism of Feminist phase protests made for better political tracts than works of art. This stage certainly represents an advance over the previous one in that it more openly identifies and contends with the oppression of women, but it too finally falls prey, through what Showalter in the introduction calls "the dependency of opposition," to dominant male power structures; obsessive criticism of these structures prevents movement beyond them into healthy, socially integrated and productive, uniquely feminine modes of thought and action (182–215).

In the final portion of her study, Showalter turns her attention to the Female phase. The book's tenth, and penultimate, chapter chronicles both the strengths and weaknesses of Virginia Woolf's version of the Female aesthetic. Drawing on Woolf's biography and fiction, Showalter contends that this influential and important Female author sought space and voice for the expression of a vision emancipated from the limitations society placed upon women, a vision in which women might share in the freedoms and privileges society afforded men. Woolf's solution was to postulate and attempt to develop an androgynous consciousness, one wholly transcending all sexual differences. As noble and progressive as this goal in many ways was, Showalter argues, it ultimately proved to be crippling and defeating. The androgynous perspective, which Woolf most fully articulated in *A Room of One's Own,* turned out not to constitute an imaginative domain "calm, stable, unimpeded by consciousness of sex," but instead to be a bloodless, frightened "escape from the confrontation with femaleness and maleness" (289). The room of one's own, image of the androgynous space projected to serve as a sanctuary for women, turned out to be a prison, isolated from real-life conflicts and conditions. Writes Showalter, "the concepts of androgyny and the private room are neither as liberating nor as obvious as they first appear. They have a darker side that is the sphere of the exile and the eunuch" (285). Again, Showalter does not merely record but also critiques, suggesting through her analysis of Woolf a form of thought that the contemporary woman should avoid.

In a 1978 review of *A Literature of Their Own,* Agate Nesaule Krause predicted that "the chapter 'Virginia Woolf and the Flight in Androgyny' is likely to be the most controversial."[16] Indeed, Showalter's representation of Woolf has elicited strong criticism. For example, Maria Ferguson has argued that "to see Woolf as a sexually afraid neurotic, whose stylistic experimentation reveals the female mode of withdrawal, is a serious misjudgment." Ferguson claims further that Showalter's reading of Woolf reveals the critic's "seeming sympathy and affirmation for traditional patriarchal commentary."[17] Nonetheless, as late as 1986, Showalter insisted on the legitimacy of the gist of what she wrote in 1977. "I would stand by much of what I said," she told an interviewer, "it just isn't all that I would say [now]."[18]

In the closing chapter, "Beyond the Female Aesthetic: Contemporary Women Novelists," Showalter examines the work of some recent Female phase authors, for example Margaret Drabble and Doris Lessing, who have attempted to surmount the shortcomings in the thought of Virginia Woolf and her contemporaries. These authors of the 1950s, 1960s, and 1970s also turn out to have their limitations, though in significant ways their texts do mark advances over those of their predecessors who "uncannily legitimized all the old stereotypes" (298). The ideal female literary stance has not yet been achieved, Showalter implies. Such a stance can only be motioned toward in the future. She implicitly sees herself as engaged in the project of raising women's consciousnesses, and thereby improving their plight, through her presentation and critiques of the female literary tradition in Britain. In the final paragraph of her book, Showalter holds out the following hope: "if women take strength in their independence to act in the world, then Shakespeare's sister, whose coming Woolf asked us to await in patience and humility, may appear at last" (319).

Showalter's second book, *The Female Malady,* is "both a feminist history of psychiatry and a cultural history of madness as a female malady."[19] Concentrating on "the psychiatric profession in England over [the last] two centuries" (5), she argues that mental illnesses of all varieties have been strongly connected with femininity. As she points out in the introduction, society "represents 'woman' *as* madness . . . uses images of the female body . . . to stand for irrationality in general" (4). Showalter's contention throughout is that these associations are culturally manufactured ideas, not objective facts of nature. The terms in which women's psychological disturbances have been conceptualized and the treatment of these maladies by the mental health profession, she maintains, reflect the patriarchal structures of a male-dominated society.

To support and illustrate her claims, Showalter relies heavily upon literature. Her book is a work of criticism firmly anchored in the premise that it is impossible to separate verbal works of art from the societies in which they were written. Texts that have

ELAINE SHOWALTER: FEMINISM

traditionally been deemed literary—poems, plays, novels, short stories—are an important and especially sensitve instrument, Showalter assumes, for recording and shaping the ideas and attitudes constituting a given culture (5–6). Throughout her book, she situates literary texts in the nest of historically specific practices and concepts that comprise the social institution she focuses upon, psychiatry. In order to understand her interpretations of these texts, it is thus necessary to examine carefully her presentation and analysis of their extraliterary settings.

The Female Malady is divided into three sections, corresponding to three major movements in British psychiatry over the past one hundred fifty years: Psychiatric Victorianism (1830–70), Psychiatric Darwinism (1870–1920), and Psychiatric Modernism (1920–80). It was in the Victorian era, Showalter contends, that women began to significantly outnumber men as psychiatric patients and that men came to be the principal caretakers of the insane (52–53). The predominant view in the Victorian period was "that women were more vulnerable to insanity than men because the instability of their reproductive systems interfered with their sexual, emotional, and rational control" (55). Various repressive efforts were made to regulate women's biological functions in order to stabilize their minds and emotions. The most extreme form these efforts took was the clitoridectomy, designed to eliminate the woman's wild, sexual urges. This operation reflected the prevalent notion of the time that female sexuality was dangerous and linked to insanity (75–78). In the asylums, "ladylike values of silence, decorum, taste, service, piety, and gratitude" were strictly enforced (79), notes Showalter. The idea behind this system of "moral management" was that if mentally ill women were forced into appropriately feminine attitudes and activities, as defined by the male establishment, they might be made "normal" (79–82).

One of the literary texts Showalter sees as best expressing and most influencing the Victorian attitude is Brontë's *Jane Eyre*. Bertha Mason, the madwoman in the attic discussed in *A Literature of Their Own*, fits the classic Victorian definition of the mentally ill woman. "Brontë offers several explanations for Bertha's madness," Showalter observes, "all taken from the discourse of Victorian psychiatry" (67). Bertha is, in keeping with the time's notion of female insanity, "a monster of sexual appetite," her illness being "linked to female sexuality and the periodicity of the menstrual cycle" (67). Showalter notes that Brontë was so trapped in the mind-set of her era that in her novel she never questions the link between insanity and female biology or feels compassion for her character. "Brontë has no sympathy for her mad creature" (69), writes Showalter. Living at a time before the advent of "moral management" techniques, Bertha is locked away at home to rave in her madness. This fictional creation's dismal plight, well known to the educated Victorian, prompted leading psychiatrists of the period such as John Conolly to argue that insane women could be better cared for in mental institutions than at home. Brontë may have had little sympathy for Bertha, but her description of this woman's treatment did have a positive effect on the course of psychiatry. "Bertha's violence, dangerousness, and rage, her regression to an inhuman condition and her sequestration," Showalter sums up Brontë's impact on medical science, "became such a powerful model for Victorian readers, including psychiatrists, that it influenced even medical accounts of female insanity" (68).

In the 1870s, in the wake of Darwin's theory of evolution, a new era in the history of mental illness was ushered in. The implications and consequences of Psychiatric Darwinism were especially pernicious for women. "Theories of biological sexual difference generated by Darwin and his disciples gave the full weight of scientific confirmation to narrow Victorian ideals of femininity" (121–22), notes Showalter. As in the Victorian period, but with greater vehemence and increased "scientific" conviction, it was argued that women were by nature mentally and psychologically inferior to men "as a result of reproductive specialization" (122). Traits deemed feminine at the time—self-sacrifice, service, passivity, patience—were seen as biological, evolutionary endowments designed to ensure "the survival and improvement of the race" (122). Women who violated their assigned roles were judged "unnatural," "crazy." The symptoms of hysteria, one of the principal forms of female mental illness during this period, included the woman's unwillingness to play the part of obedient and subservient wife and her propensity to make "selfish" demands for personal care and attention (133). The treatment for this malady centered about attempts to restore the woman to her biologically "natural" condition. The rest cure, involving physical inactivity and isolation, was designed to physiologically induce "normal" feminine behaviors of passivity and compliance (138–39).

A classic literary account of the rest cure is Charlotte Perkins Gilman's "The Yellow Wallpaper." Showalter understands this short story, which in recent years has gained wide popularity as one of the most important feminist texts of the previous century, as an artistic expression and criticism of the effects that psychiatric practices and attitudes during the Darwinian period had upon women. The narrator is a writer suffering from postpartum depression, a variety of hysteria. Her husband, a doctor, insists that a regimen of "total passivity, isolation, mental blankness" is essential to her recovery (141). Confined to an upstairs cell-like room in their house, this sensitive woman mentally disintegrates as a result of her enforced "rest." Her "blocked imaginative power" comes to fixate upon the room's yellow wallpaper, which she stares at for hours. She begins to see a female figure, the image of her trapped creative self, in the wallpaper. In a fit to free this double, she rips the paper from the wall, vainly attempting to recover her former life (142). In the end, Gilman's character "escapes into madness, making the room her refuge, creeping around its margins, and locking the door against her husband" (142). The rest cure has driven this creative and highly intelligent artist completely insane. Not only does Showalter demonstrate that Gilman uses her fiction to record and comment upon the very real horrors of a form of medical treatment popular at the time in the United States as well as in Britain, but she also establishes that this American author managed to influence, much as did Brontë in a previous generation, the historical course of psychiatry. Gilman reports in her journal, Showalter notes, that Silas Weir Mitchell, the doctor who invented the rest cure, was so moved after reading "The Yellow Wallpaper" that he altered his therapeutic approach to female psychological disturbances (141). There is a reciprocal relationship between literature and social institutions, Showalter affirms. The former shapes as well as reflects the values and practices of the latter.

At the outset of the Modernist period, which follows the Darwinian, women's mental illnesses came increasingly to be viewed as caused by environmental rather than biological factors. In the aftermath of World War I, novelists such as Rebecca West, Dorothy L. Sayers, and Virgina Woolf suggested that shell shock, a masculine malady whose symptoms mimicked those of hysteria, proved that men and women both might suffer the same psychological traumas if subjected to a similar set of intolerable circumstances (191–94).

Schizophrenia replaced hysteria as the principal female malady in the Modernist period. This disorder, still prevalent today, "offers a remarkable example of the cultural conflation of femininity and insanity" (204). Even though the majority of schizophrenics has always been male, the disease is nonetheless represented in terms of and associated with the feminine (204). Classic symptoms such as "passivity, depersonalization, disembodiment, and fragmentation," Showalter argues, "have parallels in the social situation of women" (213). In order to illustrate and substantiate the connection between women and schizophrenia, Showalter examines in detail three autobiographical novels from the early 1960s—Jennifer Dawson's *The Ha-Ha* (1961), Janet Frame's *Faces in the Water* (1961), and Sylvia Plath's *The Bell Jar* (1963). She maintains that "these novels place the blame for women's schizophrenic breakdowns on the limited and oppressive roles offered to women in modern society, and deal very specifically with institutionalization and shock treatment [popular antidotes for schizophrenia] as metaphors for the social control of women" (213). Once again, literature is interpreted in terms of its connections with the culture that produces it. Showalter understands the literary text not as an isolated, autonomous artifact, but rather as a form of social history and commentary.

The Female Malady has been criticized for forcing the connection between mental illness and the sociohistorical condition of women. "The monolithic thesis of persecution does not adequately account for the data," Patricia Meyer Spacks charges. "Women go mad, this writer believes, because society leaves them so little room. But surely one must acknowledge other— *many* other—possibilities." Spacks questions Showalter's argument that schizophrenia is inextricably tied to women's cultural plight: "To say that 'schizophrenic symptoms of passivity, depersonalization, disembodiment, and fragmentation have parallels in the social situation of women in fact says little: one might observe with equal cogency that these symptoms have parallels in the social situation of factory workers."[20]

Despite these objections, however, Showalter's book remains a provocative and innovative study, a much needed work of theory that connects literature to the history of psychiatry as interpreted from the largely neglected but crucially important angle of female interests and concerns. As H. Karp rightly judges, the book has value for a wide range of readers, potentially benefiting "students interested in women's studies, feminist therapy, and the psychology, sociology, and anthropology of women."[21]

Showalter clearly and succinctly states the subject of her next book, *Sexual Anarchy,* early in its first chapter, "Borderlines": "This book is about the myths, metaphors, and images of sexual crisis and apocalypse that marked both the late nineteenth and our own *fin de siècle,* and its representation in English and American literature, art, and film."[22] More specifically, this study, praised by Carroll Smith-Rosenberg in the *American Historical Review* as "treading new ground, opening new questions . . . a bit scandalous, certainly flamboyant, suggestive, and fun,"[23] explores in depth the destabilization of traditional notions of masculinity, femininity, and the relationship between the sexes that has occurred at the end of this century, even as it did at the close of the previous one. Some *fin de siècle* artists, past and present, welcome this destabilization; they aggressively undermine and alter previously stable sexual identities. Others, Showalter observes, see it as an enemy to be defended against; they desperately try to shore up traditional roles. In both cases, there is an awareness, consciously acknowledged or not, of the fragility of gender distinctions (10–14). It is precisely because identities can be altered that some feel such a need to reaffirm the status quo. The progressives and reactionaries alike confirm Showalter's larger thesis: masculinity and femininity are socially constructed categories, capable of being altered or reaffirmed, and not "natural, transparent, and unproblematic" essences genetically programmed into the psyche (8).

One of the principal dimensions of masculinity that is put in question, its fluidity demonstrated, by *fin de siècle* writers is sexual orientation. In chapter six, "Dr. Jekyll's Closet," Showalter examines one of the most famous nineteenth-century literary texts to engage in such questioning. Robert Louis Stevenson's *The Strange Case of Dr. Jekyll and Mr. Hyde* explores, according to Showalter, the forbidden zone of male homoeroticism, breaking through the barriers of acceptable heterosexual love into the socially proscribed domain of same-sex drives. That is, Stevenson's story attacks the socially sanctioned definition of maleness by revealing, in covert and symbolic terms, that men harbor homosexual desires. Specifically, the Jekyll-Hyde split signifies the protagonist's "need to pursue illicit sexual pleasure yet to live up to the exacting moral standards of his bleak professional community . . . " (109). Jekyll represents that portion of the doubled, conflicted self which seeks social respectability, while Hyde embodies the illicit sexual desire (109–10).

In this provocative and original reading of Stevenson's text, Showalter argues that the tale serves as a commentary on the repressed, overtly denied, sexual longings of the type of man who frequented the numerous, exclusively male clubs in existence in Britain at the turn of the century, clubs which were on the surface "aggressively and urbanely heterosexual" (12) but actually "existed on the fragile borderline that separated male bonding from homosexuality and that distinguished manly misogyny from disgusting homoeroticism" (13). *Dr. Jekyll and Mr. Hyde,* as Showalter puts it, reflects "the fantasies beneath the surface of daylight decorum, the shadow of homosexuality that surrounded Clubland and the nearly hysterical terror of revealing forbidden emotions between men that constituted the dark side of patriarchy" (107). Through Mr. Hyde and Dr. Jekyll's relationship with him, Stevenson spells out and flaunts, symbolically parades out of the closet, the latent dimension of an ambiguous and fragile masculine identity.

In the opening chapter of her book, Showalter notes that one response at the turn of the previous century to changing definitions of femininity and to increased female emancipation and influence was "the intensified valorization of male power, and expressions of anxiety about waning virility" (10). This response produced, in fact, an entire literary genre. In order to defend against assaults on masculine privilege and to escape the oppressive shadow of such powerful female authors as George Eliot, a woman whose mammoth importance and authority are the subject of chapter four of *Sexual Anarchy,* male authors invented a type of text, the masculine quest romance, which eschewed the female world entirely (76). As Showalter explains in the fifth chapter, "King Romance," the quest romance usually involved exclusively male adventures in mythical and exotic lands, locales where men could bond with each other, express their fears of and anxieties about women, and explore forbidden sexual zones in symbolic and disguised forms (81–83). These fictional realms, Showalter notes, were places where a man "might recover his virility and power" (79), which had come under assault in the real world.

In the second half of this chapter, Showalter examines in detail three masculine quest romances which appeared in the latter portion of the nineteenth century: H. Rider Haggard's *She* (1886), Rudyard Kipling's "The Man Who Would Be King" (1888), and Joseph Conrad's "Heart of Darkness" (1899). All three of these narratives "show how themes of the male muse, male bonding, and the exclusion of women came together in a complicated response to female literary dominance, as well as to British imperialism and fears of manly decline in the face of female power" (83). The text in this group which "took the genre to its artistic heights" was "Heart of Darkness" (95). Through his dismissive and sometimes fearful depictions of women, combined with his portrait of the primally masculine Kurtz and descriptions of the hypnotic bond between Kurtz and Marlow, Conrad creates a male-dominated world which is implicitly misogynist and explicitly advances masculine power, control, and solidarity (95–99).

Most of *Sexual Anarchy,* it turns out, is concerned with the literature and culture of the closing years of the nineteenth century, but Showalter does also devote sizeable space to twentieth century *fin de siècle* phenomena and to comparison of the two epochs. For example, at one point she draws parallels between "Heart of Darkness" and Francis Ford Coppola's film, *Apocalypse Now* (1979). Coppola's work, notes Showalter, is not merely an "adaptation of *Heart of Darkness*" but is instead "a contemporary mediation and interpretation, a new work that alludes to Conrad but that also can be read back into the earlier work" (99). She points out that the film faithfully reproduces most of the attitudes toward women found in the novel. In Coppola, as in Conrad, the women in the wilderness are presented as "symbolic figures of sexual danger," while the women back home "stand for a fake world of domesticity and illusion" (100). Both artists' attitudes toward women are negative, reflecting a defensive male posture. Showalter also comments on the similarities between Conrad's Marlow-Kurtz and Coppola's Willard-Kurtz relationships. In both cases there is a strong, implicitly misogynistic male bonding, with Willard's relation to Kurtz being "even more explicitly a doubling than Marlow's" (102). The point of outlining the coincidences between the film and the novel is the one announced in the first chapter of *Sexual Anarchy:* to demonstrate that treatments of gender in the two *fin de siècles* are strikingly similar.

In the final paragraph of her book, Showalter recommends lessons her readers should take from late twentieth-century sexual identity upheavals. "We must not," she insists, "allow fear to push us into a cruel homophobia, make us abandon our commitment to women's sexual autonomy, or lead us to repudiate the *fin de siècle* vision of a future in which sexuality is a source of pleasure, comfort, and joy" (207). She then projects her hopes for the next century. The anxieties and trepidations which appear "today like the apocalyptic warnings of a frightening sexual anarchy," the last sentence of her book optimistically proclaims, "may be really the birth throes of a new sexual equality" (208). The ultimate point of her study has been to suggest, through her analyses of artistic expressions at the end of both this and the previous century, attitudes toward gender and sexuality more socially and personally satisfying than those that dominated the past, attitudes that might be instituted in the future.

A collection of eight essays entitled *Sister's Choice* followed *Sexual Anarchy*. These pieces, four of which Showalter originally presented as the Clarendon Lectures at Oxford University in 1989, constitute a loosely organized history of American women's writing. As Nina Baym points out, the book "presents itself not as a master narrative but as a scrapbag assemblage."[24] This organization reflects Showalter's intention, stated in the opening chapter, "to avoid the idea that women's writing had a universal sameness that might be biological or psychological."[25] Refusing to invent artificial universalizing connections, Showalter provides relatively autonomous analyses, each of which situates particular issues and authors in the specific cultural contexts that produced them. Since the chapters of the book, which cover such diverse topics as the works of Margaret Fuller, women's interwar writings, and the female Gothic, are so loosely connected, perhaps the best way to gain a sense of Showalter's approach and to sample her insights is to examine particular essays.

The focus of the third chapter, "*Little Women:* The American Female Myth," is Louisa May Alcott and her best-known novel. Showalter argues that Alcott was torn between the desire for an independent female identity and the demands of the patriarchal culture in which she lived. She revered and respected her father, Bronson Alcott, a well-known Transcendentalist whose circle of acquaintances included Ralph Waldo Emerson, Nathaniel Hawthorne, and Henry David Thoreau. Notes Showalter, "Alcott always regarded herself as a dutiful daughter" (43). Though she read the works of American and European women writers, her early literary influences were principally the male writers her father admired, authors such as John Bunyan, Lord Byron, Sir Walter Scott, and Oliver Goldsmith (46–47). These masculine literary models, who fostered a male-centered vision of experience, ultimately proved to be "inhibiting and restrictive for an ambitious young woman writer" (47). Furthermore, Louisa found that her needs as a fledgling female author were at odds with Bronson's view of attitudes proper for a young lady. Observes Showalter, "Bronson's disapproval of female self-consciousness as selfish and narcissistic conflicted with Alcott's need to explore her own feelings as a young woman and a budding writer" (48).

This tension in Alcott between respect for and devotion to her father's masculine universe and her own needs and desires as a creative, self-directed female writer was figured into and, on

Showalter's view, successfully dealt with in *Little Women.* In the final 1880 edition of the novel, the one familiar to modern readers, the central character, Jo March, is like Alcott herself, strong and independent, a young artist who at times "gives herself up to writing with 'entire abandon,' unconscious . . . of the ordinary duties of womanhood" (58). Yet Jo also wants to avoid becoming a "'literary spinster'"; she desires the warmth and security that marriage and family offer, the sort of world Bronson Alcott represented for Louisa (58–59). In the end, Jo marries Professor Bhaer, a generous, kindhearted man, "unconfined by American codes of masculinity," who is supportive of her need to work, though not as an imaginative artist. Through her fictional character Alcott constructs a compromise, Showalter suggests, between her progressive longings for equality and personal autonomy and the traditional model of femininity endorsed by her father (58–62).

Showalter points out that many contemporary feminist critics have expressed disappointment in the protagonist's decision to marry, seeing this "domestic drama" as "a capitulation to middle-class ideals of female self-sacrifice" (57). Showalter, however, does not concur with this reading. She argues that it is wrong to demand "from Alcott's nineteenth-century female *Bildungsroman* a twentieth-century feminist ending of separation and autonomy" (57). The message of the novel was extremely progressive for its time. Showalter maintains that when viewed in historical context, "Jo's literary and emotional career is a happy one, even if it does not conform to our contemporary feminist model of a woman artist's needs" (57).

The final chapter, "Common Threads," is perhaps the most

original and interesting in *Sister's Choice*. Here Showalter considers the quilt as a distinctively feminine art form, commenting on the importance of actual quilts, quilts in literature, and the metaphorical implications of quilt making in general for American women's culture. She stresses that the meaning and significance of quilts and quilting have changed over time. And even though she sees this art form as an integral dimension of female culture, Showalter rejects the idea that quilting is a naturally feminine activity, something that women do because they are women and which men are not privy to. "While quilting does have crucial meaning for American women's texts," Showalter asserts, "it can't be taken as a transhistorical and essential form of female expression, but rather as a gendered practice that changed from one generation to the next . . . " (147).

A good example of how Showalter relates quilting to literature and demonstrates that its associations have altered through time can be seen in her discussion of Bobbie Ann Mason's 1984 story, "Love Life." The two principal characters are unmarried women of different generations. Jenny is "the New Woman of the 1980s, whose casual love affairs and backpack existence suggest the dissolution of the female world and the loss of its cultural traditions" (165). Aunt Opal, on the other hand, is a retired school teacher, an older woman "who is the caretaker of tradition" (165). When Jenny returns to her Kentucky home, she asks Aunt Opal to show her the burial quilt, a type of patchwork having its origins in the nineteenth century, which commemorates deceased family members. Intent on escaping the confining roles for women that she has grown up with and in which she is mired, Aunt Opal rejects the quilt, emblem of those traditional roles. Jenny, however, is fascinated by it, wants to learn how to make quilts herself. Alienated from female traditions, not ever having experienced their burdens, Jenny "will use the burial quilt to stitch herself back into history, to create her context" (166). For one generation of women—Aunt Opal's—the quilt is "a depressing reminder of failure, loneliness, and servitude" (166). For another generation—Jenny's—it has a completely different value; it is a sign for a currently missing sense of female continuity and community (166).

In the introduction to a recent collection of women's texts, *Daughters of Decadence,* Showalter notes that "when we think of the literature of the [nineteenth century] *fin de siècle,* the writers who come most readily to mind are men." She points out, however, that "women *were* a major presence in the new literary world of the 1880s and 1890s."[26] The point of this anthology, she declares, is "to reverse that trend [of ignoring women writers of the period] by bringing together for the first time a group of remarkable stories by English and American women at the turn of the nineteenth century."[27] Throughout her long and illustrious career, from *A Literature of Their Own,* to *Sister's Choice,* through the various collections of essays and literary texts she has edited, Showalter's overarching concern has been to surface the largely covered, repressed, and misunderstood female cultures, literary and otherwise, of America and Britain. Her aim has been to offer interpretations of these cultures which not only correct past misunderstandings and clarify women's positions in history, but also suggest, through critical interventions and projections, the course female culture might and should take in the future.

CHAPTER FIVE

Stephen Greenblatt
New Historicism

Stephen Jay Greenblatt was born on November 7, 1943 in Cambridge, Massachusetts. He received his B.A. (1964), M.Ph. (1968), and Ph.D. (1969) from Yale University. In 1966 he was awarded an A.B. and in 1969 an M.A. from Pembroke College, Cambridge. He is currently Professor of English at the University of California, Berkeley.[1] Greenblatt has edited collections of essays, published widely in leading scholarly journals, and written several major books, including *Sir Walter Ralegh: The Renaissance Man and his Roles* (1973), *Renaissance Self-Fashioning: From More to Shakespeare* (1980), *Shakespearean Negotiations: The Circulation of Social Energy in Renaissance England* (1988), *Learning to Curse: Essays in Early Modern Culture* (1990), and *Marvelous Possessions: The Wonder of the New World* (1991).

Greenblatt is a leading figure in the critical movement known as the new historicism. Begun in America in the early 1980s, this school of thought is in large measure a reaction against the tendency in much modern criticism, starting with the New Critics and extending through deconstruction, to concentrate on the language of isolated texts and ignore the worldly circumstances— the societies and times—that produced them. The new historicism returns literary works to history and culture. This return, it is important to note, does not repeat the historicism of earlier generations, which saw literature as reflecting, in mirrorlike fashion, a unified spirit of the age. Instead, it combines the urge to reconnect texts to their real-world referents and sources with the lessons of contemporary language-centered theories, which in various ways stress the power of words to make rather than merely mimic reality, in order to create a new and reinvigorated notion of literature as an historically and culturally grounded form of expression.[2]

Raman Selden identifies several specific assumptions about history, culture, and texts that underlie the work of new historicists, including Greenblatt: (1) History is not the past itself but stories about the past. The historian does not transparently reproduce events; he or she linguistically represents them, organizing and evaluating experience in terms of his or her particular ways of seeing the world. (2) There is no escaping the suppositions, the values and views, of one's own historical and cultural situation. The conceptual frameworks of those who document past and present, as well as the literary artist's imaginative vision, are shaped by their times. (3) No historical period is seamlessly unified. Each period is a composite of different, sometimes conflicting, histories. "The idea of a uniform and harmonious culture," Selden writes, "is a myth imposed on history and propagated by ruling classes in their own interests." (4) Literary and nonliterary texts are interrelated. The influence of the former can be found in the latter, and vice versa. Neither is separable from history. The literary text, like the sociological, legal, scientific, or any other sort of document, reflects and shapes, contributes to defining, the culture and period in which it was written.[3]

Greenblatt's first major new historical study, *Renaissance*

Self-Fashioning, is about the ways in which various English Renaissance writers constructed images of themselves in their texts. Viewing literary and nonliterary works as equally revealing records of the artful, literary fashionings of the self these writers engaged in, Greenblatt shuttles easily among different types of documents, not restricting himself to that which would normally be classified as literature. One of his central assumptions, which he makes clear in the introduction, is that identity-fashioning is never an act freely performed by wholly autonomous individuals. Seconding the contemporary anthropologist Clifford Geertz's observation that human beings are "cultural artifacts," Greenblatt argues that selves, then and now, are produced by "the cultural systems of meanings" in which they are necessarily embedded.[4] That is, authors shape themselves not from nothing but from the values and views which their cultures provide. This is not to say that the individual is a purely passive reflection of these values and views. People can and do modify, rebel against and otherwise manipulate, cultural resources in order to fashion their unique identities. Summing up his position in the book's brief epilogue, Greenblatt maintains that though there are "no moments of pure, unfettered subjectivity," the self being inextricably tied to its society's norms, the Renaissance writers he studies nonetheless retain at least "traces of free choice," choices they make "among possibilities whose range was strictly delineated by the social and ideological systems in force" (256).

Toward the end of the introduction, Greenblatt lists ten "governing conditions common to most instances of self-fashioning" (8–9). The gist of these conditions is "that self-fashioning occurs at the point of encounter between an authority and an alien, that what is produced in this encounter partakes of both the authority and the alien that is marked for attack, and hence that any achieved identity always contains within itself the signs of its own subversion or loss" (9). Each Renaissance author constructs himself in his text by adopting one set of values and views, produced by his culture, and rebelling against another, also culturally generated. Both the authoritative, adopted set and the alien, rejected one are elements in the composition of the author's identity. The self obviously bears the imprint of the stance it consciously seeks to assume, but it also winds up, against its will, exhibiting traits of the stance from which it vigorously attempts to disassociate. The influence of deconstruction, such as that practiced by Paul de Man, is apparent: the meaning an author intends is joined with and undermined by an opposite, contradictory meaning he does not intend. Greenblatt's Renaissance writers are ironic composites of what they want and do not want to be.

All these generalities, outlined in the introduction, are rigorously applied to specific cases in each of the book's six chapters. A single example illustrates Greenblatt's concept of self-fashioning. The second chapter of *Renaissance Self-Fashioning,* "The Word of God in the Age of Mechanical Reproduction," focuses on William Tyndale, a key Protestant figure in the sixteenth century. In such writings as *Obedience of a Christian Man* and, implicitly, through his famous vernacular translation of the Bible, Tyndale rejects the Catholic position that one can know God only through the communally held rituals and dogmas of the Catholic church, championing instead the view that each individual has the right and responsibility to form a personal relationship with God through private and prayerful reading of the Scriptures. As Greenblatt puts it, "Tyndale thus is able to reject the mediation of the church and its tradition; the individual has sufficient means within his own conscience to grasp the truth of God's word as revealed in Scripture" (99). In terms of the pattern Greenblatt describes in the introduction, Tyndale fashions himself through allegiance to an authority, in the form of Biblical revelation, and rebellion against an alien, Catholicism.

The word of God, Tyndale is clear, does not impart different meanings to different people. To read the Bible correctly is to read it literally, he maintains, and there is only one correct literal reading. Personal conscience turns out to be another name for adherence to a universal message (100). The irony of Tyndale's position is apparent. Like a good Catholic, this champion of individualism insists upon obedience to a transpersonal institution. Tyndale's institution is the literal meaning of his vernacular translation of the Bible, while the Catholic institution is the Church and its dogmas, but Book and Church alike constitute sites of self-effacement, communal receptacles into which the individual is asked to pour his or her personal devotion and private being.

The Protestant Tyndale is, in his own way, no freer from public authority than is a Catholic crusader such as Sir Thomas More, the subject of the first chapter of *Renaissance Self-Fashioning,* who staunchly holds that religious truth "is to be found only in the visible community of believers" (62). Greenblatt observes: "it [the Bible] provides for Tyndale what the church provides for More: not simply a point of vantage but a means to absorb the ambiguities of identity, the individual's mingled egotism and self-loathing, into a larger, redeeming certainty. . . . a truth that lies beyond individual or social construction. . . ." (111). As Greenblatt prescribes in the introduction, traces of the alien, which Tyndale opposes, are retained in the authority, which he upholds: his identity is an ironic composite of the Protestant position he aggressively pursues *and* the Catholic attitude he frontally attacks.

In the remaining four essays of his book, Greenblatt details the pattern of self-fashioning in Sir Thomas Wyatt, Christopher Marlowe, Edumund Spenser, and William Shakespeare. The focus of the last three chapters is more on fictional characters in texts than on the author-text relationship, but the process of self-construction is essentially the same in all. As John N. King notes, each chapter of the study "may be read as an autonomous analysis" of a particular author and his works, though "the book as a whole offers a valuable, overarching study of sixteenth-century English literature and thought."[5]

The first three chapters of Greenblatt's book deal with writers associated with Henry VIII's England, while the final three are devoted to authors connected with Elizabeth's court. In each of these triads, King observes, the progression is from an author with one particular response to "community, tradition, authority," to another with an opposite response, to a third "in which the opposition is reiterated and transformed."[6] As noted in the case of Tyndale and More, even the authors who are pitted against each other are related through ironic overlaps. Though establishing this general progression is important for Greenblatt's purposes, his central aim throughout remains the delineation of particular acts of self-fashioning, the general pattern and one example of which are sketched above.

Renaissance Self-Fashioning, which won the British Council Prize in the Humanities for the best book in British Studies by a North American scholar, was followed by *Shakespearean Negotiations,* saluted by Steven Mullaney, another prominent new historicist, as "provocative in its analyses and arguments . . . an exciting book and a generous one as well. . . ."[7] Here, as in the previous study, Greenblatt offers a theory and description of the complex relationships between literature and its social moorings. His thesis is that texts are conduits for culturally generated ideas. Authors do not express wholly original thoughts but rather draw upon a stock of common themes, contextualizing and manipulating them to serve their individual purposes. In the four essays following the introductory chapter, Greenblatt carefully traces the passage of specific ideas between texts, focussing throughout, as the title of his study indicates, on Shakespeare's plays. His strategy in each essay is to identify a particular idea, argue that Shakespeare shares it with some other author, and analyze the different uses this idea is put to, the different formulations it receives, in the playwright's and the other's texts. Greenblatt is thereby able to show that the works of William Shakespeare, so central to and venerated in the Western canon, are not the products of isolated genius but are rather intimately connected with other documents of their time, such as travelogues, histories, and religious tracts.

In "Invisible Bullets," the "most well-known of the essays"[8] in *Shakespearean Negotiations,* Greenblatt argues that a contradictory logic of simultaneous allegiance to and rejection of values and views officially endorsed by Renaissance society governs both the work of Thomas Harriot, author of an important report on the colonization of Virginia, and Shakespeare's *1 Henry IV, 2 Henry IV,* and *Henry V.* As Greenblatt explains, "understanding the relation between orthodoxy and subversion in Harriot's text will enable us to construct an interpretive model that may be used to understand the far more complex problem posed by Shakespeare's history plays."[9] This relation between orthodoxy and subversion, which constitutes a particular incarnation of what Greenblatt in the introduction calls "social energy" (6), circulates between Harriot's and Shakespeare's works, uniting these otherwise distinct cultural documents.

"In all of his extant writings, private correspondence as well as public discourse," Greenblatt observes, "Harriot professes the most reassuringly orthodox religious faith. . ." (21). *A Brief and True Report of the New Found Land of Virginia* (1588), the only work of Harriot's that appeared during his lifetime, endorses the Europeans' imposition of Christianity upon the Algonquin Indians in Virginia. Harriot outwardly upholds his religion's "intense claims to transcendence, unique truth, inescapable coercive force. . ." (30). He presents the Europeans' conquest of the natives as betokening God's blessings upon the invaders. At one point, for example, he suggests that the decimation of the Algonquins by imported Western diseases was a sign "that God protects his chosen people by killing off untrustworthy Indians" (36). Harriot confirms the might of the Christian God and declares Him to be on his culture's side by implying that God punishes those who defy his chosen people. As one who "professed belief in God" (22), Harriot was committed to the orthodox position that the Almighty defended his European emissaries to the heathen. Harriot's text also demonstrates, however, that there may be other, more unorthodox reasons why the British colonizers were able to establish dominion over the Algonquins. Though he suggests that God kills the Indians as a sign of His wrath toward them, Harriot also records certain native views that ascribed their misfortune not to God but to the Europeans themselves, one theory holding that the Europeans were "'shooting invisible bullets into them [the Indians]'" (36). This theory is, of course, uncannily close to the truth, though Harriot and his contemporaries did not realize it; the Algonquins died because of the germs—"'invisible bullets'"—their conquerors brought with them.

By objectively recording the Indians' explanation, Harriot leaves open the possibility that his Eurocentric, Christian view of the Indians' demise is not the only one available, that some other force besides divine judgment may have caused their deaths. Perhaps the power of the Christian God is not real but merely a propaganda tool for scaring the natives into compliance, Harriot's text inadvertently suggests. God and His wrath may merely be myths, employed to justify European conquest and to convince the Indians they should convert and obediently go along with their invaders' program (36–37). Harriot, in short, lapses into heresy. *A Brief and True Report* contains "the very core of the Machiavellian anthropology that posited the origin of religion in an imposition of socially coercive doctrines by an educated and sophisticated lawgiver on a simple people" (27). Harriot's text is at once subversive and orthodox, undermining the authenticity and divinely sanctioned authority of the Christian faith it purports to uphold. It is crucial to note, however, that this report attempts to control and contain the subversion it expresses; the implicitly heretical views are introduced in the service of the orthodox position the text means to confirm. Harriot records the Indians' explanations only in order to present their culture for European "study, discipline, correction, transformation" (37). His intention in registering alien voices is not to demonstrate that there is more than one truth, but rather to define the Indians' views, to sketch a portrait of their culture, so that it will be clear exactly who these people are and why they need to be instructed in the truth of Christianity (37). Nonetheless, the subversiveness remains, available to the perceptive reader and always threatening to undo the orthodox Christian view Harriot explicitly promotes.

In the second half of "Invisible Bullets," Greenblatt turns his attention to Shakespeare's treatment of political power in the history plays. His argument is that these dramas at once celebrate King Henry's majesty and denounce it as ill-gotten. Greenblatt points out, for example, that in *I Henry IV* Prince Hal uses tricks and deception to rise to the position of trusted, honored leader. "We are continually reminded," Greenblatt writes, "that Hal is a 'juggler,' a conniving hypocrite, and that the power he both serves and comes to embody is glorified usurpation and theft" (41). Hal establishes himself as a good and decent man by turning on the low-life tavern companions, most prominently Falstaff, who in the beginning were his close friends and allies. Honorable Hal, notes Greenblatt is "the prince and principle of falsification—he is himself a counterfeit companion. . ." (42). Similarly, in *Henry V* evil is purged from the state with evil; the prince's glory is achieved through inglorious acts: "The play deftly registers every nuance of royal hypocrisy, ruthlessness, and bad faith—testing, in effect, the proposition that successful rule depends not upon sacredness but upon demonic violence—but it does so in the context of a celebration, a collective panegyric to 'This star of England,' the charismatic leader who purges the commonwealth of its incorrigibles and forges the martial national state" (56).

The contradictory logic of orthodoxy and subversion is apparent. On the one hand, the plays affirm the socially sanctioned power and authority that Prince Hal rises to embody. In politically correct fashion, they approvingly highlight his outward glory and honor and applaud his benevolent rule. At the same time, however, Shakespeare severely undermines Hal's goodness. He heretically demonstrates that the prince's virtues and status are unscrupulously and wickedly acquired. It is essential to realize that this attack of the monarchy is conducted entirely within the confines of its support. Hal's hypocrisy, his pretense of being wholly admirable and without blame, works to promote his authority at the same time that it hides his sinister, despicable side from the audience. Thus, though Shakespeare's plays both orthodoxly affirm the crown and subversively defame it, the defamation is cloaked in and controlled by the affirmation.

What Shakespeare has done is repeat the central, structuring idea of Harriot's *A Brief and True Report.* To be sure, the playwright employs the logic of orthodoxy and subversion in a different context and to serve different ends than does the historian: while the former shows that it is at work in the monarch's acquisition and implementation of political power, the latter demonstrates that these contradictory principles govern the transmission and maintenance of the Christian faith. Nevertheless, these very different texts are connected by this single logic; both Shakespeare and Harriot affirm and assault a cultural orthodoxy, the assault being uneasily incorporated into and always threatening to unravel the affirmation it is used to bolster. Greenblatt's point, it should be noted, is not that either Shakespeare or Harriot is the original source of this logic, which is the concrete expression of amorphous cultural anxieties concerning power and authority. To the contrary, his claim is that the idea of orthodoxy and subversion is a cultural resource that both writers draw upon, each modifying and shaping it in his own terms.

In "Shakespeare and the Exorcists," the fourth chapter of *Shakespearean Negotiations,* Greenblatt, as David Norbrook notes, "explores the boundaries between the sacred and the secular."[10] Samuel Harsnett's *A Declaration of Egregious Popish Impostures* is used to illustrate the sacred, while the representative secular text is Shakespeare's *King Lear.* This exploration amounts to an analysis, as in "Invisible Bullets," of the connection between apparently unrelated documents. "The relation between these two texts [*A Declaration* and *Lear*]," Greenblatt states at the outset, "enables us to glimpse with unusual clarity and precision the institutional negotiation and exchange of social energy" (94). Each text is a unique articulation of a single, culturally generated idea: demon possession and exorcisms are not real but rather illusions.

Harsnett, a defender of the Church of England, sets out to debunk exorcisms, which were performed primarily by the Catholic clergy, in order to cancel potential competition with Anglican authority. His feeling is that these spectacles channel religious fervor away from "the sole legitimate possessor of absolute charismatic authority, the monarch, Supreme Head of the Church of England" (97). By focussing on the exorcist's feats, people tend to forget, he believes, that religious power resides with the King, not with the exorcists. Harsnett's strategy is to show exorcisms to be pure theater, fictions enacted by players on a stage. He "is determined to make the spectators [of exorcisms] see the theater around them, to make them understand that what seems spontaneous is rehearsed, what seems involuntary carefully crafted, what seems unpredictable scripted" (106). If people realize that demon possession and exorcisms are lies, then they will no longer be fascinated by them and will turn their attention where it belongs, to the King. It is important to note that in showing up exorcisms as fakes, as theater, Harsnett does not simply make the demonic disappear. Rather, he transfers it from the subject being exorcised to the cleric performing the exorcism. Those who perpetrate the "chicanery and delusion" (99) of exorcisms, he argues, are, if not exactly demon possessed, nonetheless emissaries of Satan (97–98).

In *King Lear,* Shakespeare "stages not only exorcism, but Harsnett *on* exorcism. . ." (116). His play is a fictional, dramatic rendition of truths about exorcism that Harsnett presents in didactic, expository form. Shakespeare, for example, provides a character, Edgar, who appears to be demon possessed but who in actuality, as the audience realizes, is only pretending. That is, he reiterates Harsnett's truth that demon possession is a fraud; Edgar, like those exorcised by Catholic clerics, is not really possessed, and the play's spectators, like the reader's of Harsnett's book, are made aware that possession is merely good theater (117–18). Likewise, when Edgar tells the blind, psychologically tormented Gloucester that he has witnessed a demon depart from him, the theatergoers, like Edgar, are cognizant of the ruse. Edgar is lying, the audience knows, in a benevolent attempt "to create in Gloucester an experience of awe and wonder so intense that it can shatter his suicidal despair and restore his faith in the benevolence of the gods. . ." (118). Shakespeare is presenting on stage Harsnett's claim that the dismissal of demons is not real but mere playacting.

It is important to note that these Shakespearean representations are not exact and entirely faithful duplications of Harsnett. In staging his predecessor Shakespeare transforms him: "Harsnett's arguments are alienated from themselves when they make their appearance on the Shakespearean stage. . . . the closer Shakespeare seems to a source. . . . the more devastating and decisive his transformation of it" (120).

This alienation and transformation stem from Shakespeare's emptying *all* supernatural substance from the theater of demon possession. Whereas Harsnett relocates the demonic from the exorcised to the exorcist, Shakespeare cancels the demonic altogether. Whereas Harsnett switches divine sanction from the act of exorcism to the King of England, Shakespeare erases all holy authority. The play makes it clear that neither devils nor gods really exist, though it repeatedly excites a desire for them. Both Edgar's possession and Gloucester's purging are theater only, neither staging intended to defend a religious institution or denounce a Satanic one. Shakespeare, notes Greenblatt, "writes for the greater glory and profit of the theater, a fraudulent institution that never pretends to be anything but fraudulent. . ." (127). That is, the playwright celebrates precisely what Harsnett denounces: pretense, stagings. "The force of *King Lear,*" Greenblatt concludes, "is to make us love the theater, to seek out its satisfactions, to serve its interests, to confer on it a place of its own, to grant it life by permitting it to reproduce itself over generations" (127).

Diverse cultural documents, Shakespeare's tragedy and Harsnett's expository tract, are united by the single idea that exorcisms and demon possession are frauds. This idea is altered as it circulates between the two texts. Harsnett uses the notion that possession and exorcism are only theater to defend one religious viewpoint and attack another, while Shakespeare employs it to cancel the supernatural altogether and celebrate pure theatrics. As in "Invisible Bullets" and the other essays in *Shakespearean Negotiations,* Greenblatt shows that neither Shakespeare's plays nor the works to which it is being compared are the isolated creations of an autonomous author. Rather, each text is structured and informed by common material, generated by the culture at large, which each author treats in his unique way.

Learning to Curse, like *Shakespearean Negotiations,* is a collection of essays representing Greenblatt's work over the past twenty years; the oldest of the pieces, "Learning to Curse: Aspects of Linguistic Colonialism in the Sixteenth Century," first appeared in 1976. Though he declares in the book's opening sentence that these essays "do not tell a unified story," he also adds that they do "describe an intellectual trajectory."[11] This trajectory extends through such diverse subjects as the application of psychoanalysis to Renaissance literature ("Psychoanalysis and Renaissance Culture"), ritual urine drinking ("Filthy Rites"), and demarcation of the wilderness in Yosemite park

STEPHEN GREENBLATT: NEW HISTORICISM

("Towards a Poetics of Culture"). "The strengths of Greenblatt's historicism are beyond question," Terry Eagleton asserts in a *Times Literary Supplement* review of the book. "More than almost any other contemporary critic, he has restored our sense of works of art as material events, palpable interventions in reality rather than pale reflections of it."[12] Eagleton's observation suggests the path of the "intellectual trajectory" that the pieces in *Learning to Curse* describe, a trajectory that Greenblatt himself outlines in the introduction. Greenblatt tells the story of his rejection of the New Critics' exclusive emphasis, which he was taught at Yale in the 1960s, on the isolated, autonomous text, and his turn toward the socially engaged criticism he learned under the tutelage of Raymond Williams, a leading marxist theorist, at Cambridge (1–2). He relates this personal odyssey "precisely because it is not entirely personal. . ."(3). He sees himself as a participant in a "general tendency, a shift away from a criticism centered on 'verbal icons' toward a criticism centered on cultural artifacts" (3). That is, he is one of many who has begun to understand texts in terms of the historical periods and cultures which they shape and are shaped by. In the early portion of his career, he relates, he conceived of this shift "as a turn to Marxist aesthetics," but in recent years, "in the wake of an interest in anthropology and post-structuralism," he has come to think of his practice as "'cultural poetics' or 'new historicism'" (3). The essays in *Learning to Curse* theorize about and engage in depth this practice, a practice already under way in his first two books.

In "Learning to Curse," Greenblatt explores the cultural chauvinism underlying European attitudes toward New World Indian languages. Prior to the eighteenth century, two positions prevailed. On the one hand, there were those who argued that the Indians were essentially without language, at least a language that "civilized" men might comprehend and use. Observes Greenblatt, "the view that Indian speech was close to gibberish remained current in intellectual as well as popular circles at least into the seventeenth century" (19). On the other hand, there were those who believed that there was essentially no difference between Indian and European tongues, that Indian speech could be easily and directly translated into European idioms. "Again and again in the early accounts, Europeans and Indians, after looking on each other's faces for the first time, converse without the slightest difficulty" (27), Greenblatt remarks. "There were interpreters, to be sure, but these are frequently credited with linguistic feats that challenge belief" (27).

On the surface, these two views would appear to be diametrically opposed; however, on a deeper level, they sponsor the same prejudiced, Eurocentric vision. As Greenblatt analyses the mindset of the colonialists, Europeans saw their ways of thinking and being, represented by and expressed through their languages, as constituting the one, "true" reality. The Indians were either relegated to the status of wild men, lacking access to the colonizers' language and thus to all civilized society, or were viewed as primitive Europeans, who spoke essentially the same language as their invaders and thus participated in the same basic reality, albeit a cruder version of it, the Indians being in need of the refinements and instruction the invading civilization had to offer (16–30).

The problem with both positions, as Greenblatt sees it, is that they "reflect a fundamental inability to sustain the simultaneous perception of likeness and difference. . ." (31). Europeans could not entertain the possibility that there might be a distinctively Indian civilization worthy of recognition and respect, one which overlapped with European civilization in certain respects but which also exhibited its own, peculiar features reflecting an alternative reality. In the European mind, Greenblatt sums up his analysis, the Indians were pushed either "toward utter difference—and thus silence—or toward utter likeness—and thus the collapse of their own, unique identity" (31).

Greenblatt carefully figures a literary text, Shakespeare's *The Tempest,* and several nonliterary texts, for instance, Ralegh's *History of the World* and the Spanish *Requeriminto,* into this discussion of linguistic colonialism, explaining how these works, in different ways, broach and treat this cultural theme. He follows the new historical principle of situating texts in the nest of material and social forces which produced them, refusing to treat them, as would a New Critic, as if they were wholly autonomous, isolated documents.

In the book's final essay, "Resonance and Wonder," Greenblatt continues to maintain that written works are embedded in contexts, but he sounds a somewhat different note by stressing that texts cannot be understood *solely* in terms of how they connect with society and history. In this piece he openly expresses a healthy respect, implicit in all his work, for the power and uniqueness of the individual work of art. Greenblatt's avowal in the introduction to move away from the New Critics' exclusive concentration on the isolated text does not entail denying that it is possible or sometimes profitable to view works of art in isolation.

Greenblatt couches this respect for the individual art work in a historical and cultural context. He recognizes the fact that one of the ways different societies at different points in time have viewed art is in terms of its power to arrest attention apart from its historical and cultural conditions. The argument revolves around a distinction between the two terms of the essay's title. Greenblatt defines "resonance" as the ability of a work of art "to reach out beyond its formal boundaries to a larger world, to evoke in the viewer the complex, dynamic cultural forces from which it has emerged. . ." (170). Wonder, in contrast, signifies the work's power "to stop the viewer in his tracks, to convey an arresting sense of uniqueness, to evoke an exalted attention" (170). To experience the resonance of a composition is to understand it in terms of the cultural context in which it was produced and that it reflects. To be captivated by wonder involves perceiving the art object as highly original, unique, and self-contained. "[W]hen the act of attention draws a circle around itself from which everything but the object is excluded," wonder emerges (176).

Modern art museums, Greenblatt notes, highlight the wonder of art works by isolating them for viewing: "the heart of the mystery lies with the uniqueness, authenticity, and visual power of the masterpiece, ideally displayed in such a way as to heighten its charisma, to compel and reward the intensity of the viewer's gaze, to manifest artistic genius" (178). He concludes that artistic texts, whether they be written or pictorial, should be mined for their wonder as well as for their resonance.

Perhaps the most interesting and complex of the essays in *Learning to Curse* is "Towards a Poetics of Culture." Greenblatt begins by noting that he coined the term "new historicism" in the introduction to a collection of essays for *Genre* (146). He then proposes to "try if not to define the new historicism, at least to situate it as a practice—a practice rather than a doctrine, since as far as I can tell (and I should be the one to know) it's no doctrine at all" (146).

H. Aram Veeser points out that one of the charges commonly levelled against new historicists from the political right is that their projects are simply warmed-over versions of Marxism. Veeser, however, insists that "New Historicism is as much a reaction against Marxism as a continuation of it."[13] Greenblatt defines his practice precisely by relating it to and distinguishing it from pure Marxism, situating it in the intersection between Marxist and poststructuralist theory. Greenblatt's argument is, in brief, as follows. Poststructuralist theorists, such as Jean François Lyotard, see Western capitalist culture as attempting artificially to reduce the chaos of radically distinct ideas and philosophies comprising it to a single, unified world view reflecting capitalist values and economic conditions. That is, the capitalist system pressures its thinkers into seeing everything—all attitudes and actions—as ultimately connected to and consonant with capitalism. In Lyotard's own words, "'capital is that which wants a single language [way of organizing and thinking about reality] and a single network, and it never stops trying to present them'" (149). Marxist theorists, such as Fredric Jameson, maintain exactly the opposite, that capitalism fosters a seeming multiplicity of radically distinct perspectives that can and should be intergrated in a single, unified vision grounded in sociopolitical values and economic conditions. Every idea, no matter how remote from capitalist values and economic conditions it may on the surface appear to be, is ultimately rooted in them and bears their impress, Jameson argues (147–48).

Greenblatt is critical of both positions, maintaining that the poststructuralist and Marxist visions alike are distorted, partial and simplistic. Contemporary capitalist culture, he contends, demonstrates *both* the desire to collapse all ideas and perspectives—discourses—into one, *and* an impulse to produce radically distinct ideas and perspectives that cannot be so reduced. In Greenblatt's words: "For capitalism has characteristically generated neither regimes in which all discourses seem coordinated, nor regimes in which they seem radically isolated or discontinuous, but regimes in which the drive toward differentiation and the drive toward monological organization operate simultaneously, or at least oscillate so rapidly as to create the impression of simultaneity" (151). Greenblatt's vision is a complex one, detecting in deconstructive fashion contradictory tendencies operative in a single phenomenon.

Marvelous Possessions, Greenblatt's next book, was praised by Simon Schama in the *New Republic* as "by far the most intellectually gripping and penetrating discussion of the relationship between intruders and natives [to appear in recent years]."[14] Here Greenblatt examines in detail a subject he has raised in previous texts: "early European responses to the New World."[15] This study, he projects in the introduction, will concentrate on the analysis of anecdotes rather than larger narrative structures that organize a multitude of facts into some general, overarching framework. The anecdote, a characteristic concern of new historicists in general and already a prominent interest in Greenblatt's earlier books, registers "the locally real" and "the singularity of the contingent" (3). This literary mode is an especially important feature of travel discourses of the late Middle Ages and Renaissance, the principal focus of *Marvelous Possessions,* because such discourses are "rarely if ever interesting" as coherent, chronologically progressive accounts of foreign adventures, their fascination lying instead in their records of particular, isolated events and experiences (2). Greenblatt adds that the anecdote suggests "a larger progress or pattern"; the particulars it registers reflect general cultural attitudes and values (3). By centering on the anecdote, he will thus be able to uncover representative European perspectives as he examines specific encounters with foreign lands and peoples.

Wonder, Greenblatt declares, is "the central figure in the initial European response to the New World . . ." (14). All the anecdotes he analyses concerning both the New World and other portions of the globe convey this figure, which is related to but has broader implications than the wonder delineated in "Resonance and Wonder." This concept is defined in the introduction as "the decisive emotional and intellectual experience in the presence of radical difference . . ." (14). Though prompted by external, real-world facts, wonder is itself a deeply personal and inward feeling. It entails the way individuals, stamped by the customs and values of their cultures, are impacted by the customs and values of other cultures.

One might easily object to Roberto González Echevarría's charge in the *New York Times Book Review* that Greenblatt's book lacks a "fully articulated purpose."[16] That purpose, amply fulfilled in the four chapters comprising *Marvelous Possessions,* is the investigation of the senses of wonder different European explorers experienced in the strange and marvelous worlds they visited.

The first chapter, "From the Dome of the Rock to the Rim of the World," is concerned with the treatment of wonder in a fourteenth-century narrative of discovery, *Mandeville's Travels*. Greenblatt begins by pointing out that Sir John Mandeville was "an unredeemable fraud," many of his so-called eyewitness accounts having been stolen from other sources (31). He further notes that the author's identity—where he came from, who exactly he was—has been called into question by scholars in recent years (33). These facts, however, do not detract from the value of his text as a record of one of the ways in which Europeans reacted to exotic peoples and places. Mandeville's predominant stance, Greenblatt observes, is one of "renunciation." He refuses "to take possession" of, "to occupy," the marvelous regions he reports exploring (27). "[I]n contrast to Marco Polo, who is constantly weighing the possibilities for trade, and to Columbus, who imagines that he is acquiring for his sovereigns an outlying corner of the great Khan's empire, Mandeville takes possession of nothing" (26).

His respect for other cultures is noteworthy. In the anecdotal accounts of wonders recorded in the second half of his book, Mandeville simultaneously connects his society with foreign ones and distances it from them. "Each point in the world," he theorizes, "is balanced by an antipodean point to which it is at once structurally linked and structurally disjoined" (43). He recognizes that the habits and customs of other races are similar to as well as different from his own. The effect of this double

vision is to deauthorize European values and views as the single
standard by which the truth of all other cultures' practices are
judged. Mandeville, for the most part, refuses to colonize—
"possess"—alien perspectives by eliding them with his own or
condemning them as false and evil and thereby justifying their
replacement by European forms of thought. To the contrary, he
faithfully registers and tolerantly accepts points of difference,
fully acknowledging the validity of divergent outlooks.

For example, at one point Mandeville describes a Tibetan
burial ritual which entails the dismemberment and eating, by both
birds and relatives, of the corpse. Greenblatt notes that in
Mandeville's analysis this radically different custom shares
"structural parallels with the Christian practice of transforming
parts of saintly bodies into artifacts, with pious rituals of remembrance, and with a eucharistic piety that ardently celebrated the
eating of the sacred flesh and the drinking of the sacred blood"
(45). Mandeville, in short, recognizes in the native practice "the
parabolic quality of otherness . . . its inverted, metaphoric
representation of the central rituals of Christian culture. . ." (45).

Acknowledging parallels between others' customs and his
own leads him to conclude that the differences—the "inver-
sions"—which arise out of these similarities signal that there is
not just one truth but many. Europeans, Mandeville implies, have
their version of cannibalism and the transformation of body parts
into hallowed artifacts, expressed in Holy Communion and the
veneration of saints, while those in another culture have theirs, in
the form of burial rituals. The Christian-European version is no
less barbaric, no more meaningful or legitimate, than that of the
pagan aliens. Seeing the familiar in the other and the other in the

familiar illuminates the relative merits of each. Greenblatt concludes: "Mandeville passes from a possessive insistence on the core orthodox Christian belief to an open acceptance of many coexisting beliefs" (45).

As noted, Christopher Columbus, unlike his predecessor Mandeville, makes no pretence of renunciation; in fact, he is intent upon fully possessing the New World he discovers. In his extensive travel journals, which Greenblatt discusses in detail in the second chapter of *Marvelous Possessions,* Columbus records his formal, written declaration of ownership, in the name of the Spanish crown, of the islands he first sets foot on in 1492 (54). Spanish law provides that objection to possession may be claimed. But since the natives "are not in the same universe of discourse" as their Western invaders, they are incapable of registering such an objection; these mysterious others are not familiar with European laws or notions of ownership, do not speak the same language, and thus have no inkling of their right to formal protest (59). That the natives could not possibly know to object to an alien, incomprehensible proclamation of seizure is absolutely irrelevant to Columbus. As Greenblatt notes, the Spanish conqueror exhibits a "complete indifference to the consciousness of the other" (59). In essence what Columbus does is presume that the one and only discourse is the European discourse and since the natives do not participate in it, they are hardly human, the taking of their property being of as little consequence and as justified as marauding an animal's habitat (60).

Later, when the islands are actually captured, Columbus sees his invasion as a benevolent service to the Indians. In the spirit of what Greenblatt labels "Christian imperialism," Columbus maintains that by enslaving the Indians he is enabling their emancipation from "their own bestiality" and providing for their conversion to the one, true faith (70). The rhetoric of wonder—the description of the natives as exotic, savage beasts in need of "civilizing"—serves to justify this brutalizing conquest of the New World. In Greenblatt's words: "The production of wonder then is not only an expression of the effect that the voyage had upon Columbus but a calculated rhetorical strategy, the evocation of an aesthetic response in the service of a legitimation process" (73–74).

Greenblatt closes *Marvelous Possessions* by recounting an anecdote from his own travels. Once while in a village church in Mexico, he observed a carved figure of the crucified Jesus, above which loomed a stone image of the Mixtec god of death. Greenblatt writes: "The image [of the Mixtec god] looked down directly at the face of the crucified god. The divinities have exchanged this sightless gaze, this perpetual circulation, for more than four hundred years" (151).

This picture of radically opposed yet intimately connected religious icons is a fitting conclusion to this book about the collusions and conflicts between invaded and invading cultures. It also serves as an apt image for Greenblatt's work as a whole, from *Renaissance Self-Fashioning* to *Marvelous Possessions,* which is devoted to measuring the intersections and divergences among culturally specific values, beliefs, and forms of expression.

CHAPTER SIX

Edward W. Said
Political Critique

Edward W. Said was born in Jerusalem, Palestine, on November 1, 1935.[1] His family immigrated to Egypt in 1947, where he studied in British schools.[2] At age fifteen he entered an American boarding school. From there he went to Princeton, graduating with an A.B. in 1957 and an A.M. in 1960, and then to Harvard, where he received his Ph.D. in 1964.[3] As well as being a distinguished literary theorist and critic, Said has "for more than twenty years been the most visible spokesperson for the Palestinian cause in the United States. . . ."[4] He is presently University Professor at Columbia University.

In a 1986 interview, Said observes that "the sense of being between cultures has been very, very strong for me. I would say that's the single strongest strand running through my life: the fact that I'm always in and out of things, and never really *of* anything for very long."[5] It is not surprising, then, that the impulse to transgress boundaries, to intermix normally segregated domains in order to show how each is intertwined with others, is as central to Said's approach as it is to Henry Louis Gates's.

In his recent, most influential work, Said, like Stephen Greenblatt, views literary and nonliterary texts alike as documents that reflect and mold the cultures and historical periods in which they were written. His transgressive impulse translates into an effort to connect texts with each other and with their real world circumstances, rather than, in New Critical fashion, to analyse them in isolation. "What is interesting about literature, and everything else, is the degree to which it's mixed with other things, not its purity,"[6] he says. And in a later interview he adds: "I am of the rather strong persuasion that all texts—and the texts that interest me most are the ones that are most this way—all texts are mixed in some way."[7] To read Said's work is to be cast in the role of the migrant, never at home in a single place but always shuttling among different textual, social, and historical provinces.

Said connects texts with each other and society in order to make political points. Perhaps more consistently and urgently than any of the other five theorists in this book, he has, especially since the publication of *Orientalism* in 1978, attempted to uncover complicities between artistic productions and state power, to critique dominant social institutions and the value-laden images they produce. Said sees himself, sometimes explicitly and always implicitly, as attempting through his texts to make a real world difference, as contributing to the creation of a more humane and tolerant international community.

The major problem in presenting Said's theory and criticism is the bulk of his writing. Since it is impossible to canvas all his many books and essays in a brief chapter such as this, four representative, widely known works in literary/critical circles will be examined: *Beginnings: Intention and Method* (1975), *Orientalism* (1978), *The World, the Text, and the Critic* (1983), and *Culture and Imperialism* (1993). In *Beginnings,* unlike in his later works, Said expressly sets out to avoid political and social issues. The book, as the title indicates, is a study of the act of creation. More specifically, it is an examination of how and why authors begin new texts. Said's exploration of this subject, which is the exclusive concern of the first two chapters, "Beginning Ideas" and "A Meditation on Beginnings," comes to serve as a platform for considering a wide range of literary/critical issues, many of which are only circuitously related to the notion of beginnings. This is perhaps most noticeably true in the lengthy fifth chapter, "*Abecedarium Culturae:* Absence, Writing, Statement, Discourse, Archaeology, Structuralism," which provides a detailed account of current—in 1975—trends in literary theory. *Beginnings,* in sum, serves as a useful introduction to major issues and figures which have shaped the background for critical theory in the 1990s, as well as offering an original, influential analysis of textual origins.

Said's far-reaching observations on beginnings in the first two chapters center about three key points. (1) The beginnings he is concerned with are linguistic. He purposefully plays down the "historical-political circumstances" of texts, opting instead for "*the history and coherence of beginnings as a fact of written language. . . .*as opposed to the history and coherence of social reality. . . ."[8] His assumption is that though literature and critical languages are certainly connected to history, society, and politics, they nonetheless constitute a separate realm which operates according to its own, distinct laws. "To begin to write," Said notes, "is to work a set of instruments. . ." (24). Those instruments are the grammar and vocabulary of language, the system of rules and regulations for combining words to create meaning. Literature, one of Said's principal concerns, employs language according to the dictates of literary conventions and traditions to create artificial, self-contained, fictional universes (10–11).

(2) Said asserts that a beginning always implies an authorial intention. Though a writer must always operate from within the confines of the vocabulary, grammar, and conventions provided by language, it is the writer's conscious aim, not the autonomous and anonymous linguistic system, that creates his or her text. Said writes: "to begin to apprehend a text is to begin to find intention and method in it—not, in other words, to reduce a text to a continuous stream of words emanating from a disembodied causal voice. . ." (59). Writers purposefully manipulate language, beginning new texts by consciously choosing to use words to achieve particular ends.

(3) What every author—be he or she a "creative" writer (novelist, poet, dramatist) or a critic—intends in his or her beginning is difference from everyone else's writing. "Beginnings inaugurate a deliberately *other* production of meaning. . ." (13), says Said. "With regard to what precedes it, a beginning represents . . . a discontinuity. . ." (34). To begin a text is to do things with words that other writers have not already done, to deploy the concepts and conventions provided by language in fresh and original ways.

In the third chapter of *Beginnings,* Said turns his attention to the novel. This genre, he argues, has two "*beginning* conditions": authority and molestation (83). Authority is an individual author's impulse and power to create something new, his or her drive to produce "an increase over what had been there previously" (83). Molestation describes the relationship between the text and the world. The novel "molests" reality in that it transforms it into language and literary conventions, creating a fictive universe that is something very different from the real world the text is purportedly about. Molestation "occurs when novelists and critics traditionally remind themselves of how the novel is always subject to a comparison with reality and thereby found to be illusion" (84).

Said uses Joseph Conrad's *Nostromo* to illustrate in detail how these dual beginning conditions operate in the case of a particular modern novel. His argument is that Conrad, much more than most novelists who preceded him, is acutely, painfully aware of the fact and implications of molestation. *Nostromo* expresses "loss of faith in the ability of novelistic representation directly to reflect anything except the author's dilemmas. . ." (137). Conrad's desire to create something new—his authority— ends in "a revulsion from the novelist's whole procreative enterprise and an intensification of his *scriptive* fate" (137). What Conrad discovers and implicitly demonstrates in his novel is that the writer is hopelessly immersed in the play of language and literary conventions, absolutely unable to escape into satisfying and efficacious commentary upon the real world. This early twentieth-century author comes to the conclusion that to begin a novel is to work with verbal resources, not objective facts.

The fifth and penultimate chapter of *Beginnings* provides what Wesley A. Morris, in a 1976 review, calls an "extremely valuable and much needed" critique of structuralism.[9] Said accepts certain structrualist assumptions but dissents from a crucial conclusion. He endorses the idea that writing creates rather than merely imitates reality. Meaning, the structuralists argue, is not built into the world but rather foisted upon it, produced by the system of concepts language conveys. The

EDWARD W. SAID: POLITICAL CRITIQUE

words and syntax of sentences order and structure the world, making sense of raw data (315–33). It should be noted that this view is somewhat at odds with Said's contention in chapter one that language can be separated from society and politics. For structuralists, the linguistic, social, and political blend into each other, language being seen as defining and reflecting the politically stratified societies that generate it.

In the course of illuminating and promoting the idea that words make the world, Said gives an extensive and highly useful summary of the work of such key figures associated with structuralism as Michel Foucault, Claude Levi-Strauss, and Roland Barthes. At the time *Beginnings* was published, these writers were just beginning to be widely read by American critics and have an impact on their work. Among the many merits of this chapter is its introduction of the thought of some of the most important and influential theorists on the contemporary scene.

An important corollary of the general claim that language constitutes reality is the idea that the human subject is the product of the words it uses. People see themselves—they define their values, views, and environment—not just any way they choose but rather as the system of concepts provided by their language allows (288). For instance, when one describes an individual as a man, one draws upon definitions of the word "man" that contemporary English makes available. It is only because the concept "man" is contained in the language that one is able to think of another person, or oneself, in these terms.

In Foucault's analysis, writes Said, the self "is dissolved in the overarching waves, in the quanta and striations of language itself, turning finally into little more than a constituted subject, a speaking pronoun, fixed indecisively in the eternal, ongoing rush of discourse" (287). All structuralists share a sense of man as hopelessly "mired . . . in his systems of signification" (319); people's thoughts and actions, their very identities, are determined by the terms of their language. The conviction that the self is shaped by language leads some structuralists to discount individual authorial will and intention entirely. They see the writer as doing nothing more than passively mouthing already in-place ways of looking at the world. The possibility of beginnings is effectively cancelled. Texts do not initiate their authors' original visions, but merely continue ways of conceptualizing experience embedded in language (318–19).

As is clear from the opening chapter of *Beginnings,* Said rejects this conclusion. While he agrees that language necessarily shapes the self and its sense of reality, that there is finally no way of getting outside established conceptual systems, he nonetheless retains a belief in the self's ability to project new thoughts, to begin new texts. "A major criticism of the structuralists is," Said asserts, "that the moving force of life and behavior, the *forma informans,* intention, has been, in their work, totally domesticated by system. This, I believe, is a consequence of gravely underestimating the rational potency of the beginning, which to them is an embarrassment for systematic thought" (319–20). In Said's view, unlike that of many of the structuralists, the writer has the power to manipulate, to shape and direct, language in his or her unique, personal terms.

Said's model, introduced in the final chapter, is the eighteenth-century Italian philosopher Giambattista Vico, who, as John Kucich explains, sees authors as bound by "traditional knowledge and cultural limits" yet possessing a "nearly infinite capacity for discontinuous invention."[10] Said also endorses Foucault's belief in the possibility of resisting established ways of looking at the world from within the confines of those perspectives. Though the French philosopher holds, in keeping with the structuralist vision, that people are indeed "dissolved in the overarching waves, in the quanta and striations of language itself," he nonetheless assumes, contra many structuralists, that authors can reinterpret those terms, criticize and revise them, to serve their own, personal purposes. For Foucault, Said notes approvingly, writing can be an "act of taking hold of language (*prendre la parole*) in order to do something, not merely in order to repeat an idea verbatim" (378).

This Foucauldian "taking hold of language," like Vico's "discontinuous invention," marks the possibility and point of beginning. "A major thesis of this book," Said, repeating his earlier contention, states toward the end, "is that beginning is a consciously intentional, productive activity..." (372). Though he situates authors within language, insisting with the structuralists that the self is shaped by the concepts provided by extant systems of thought, he never relinquishes his conviction that individual writers can create something new, can initiate fresh beginnings by imaginatively doing things with and to language that have never been done before.

Though there are many parallels between *Beginnings* and Said's next book, *Orientalism,* there are also some profound differences, the most obvious of which is that the sociopolitical dimension of texts expressly avoided in the opening chapters of the former work becomes the primary focus of the latter. Said's argument in *Orientalism* is that the Western concept of the Orient has been manufactured by the distorting, pernicious terms in which Western scholars and artists have come to talk about this region of the world, by the ways their discourses have denigrated rather than charitably presented it. In the course of this three hundred fifty page study, Said meticulously details these distorting discourses as they have developed over the years, explaining how and for what purposes one culture has created another. The implicit point of the book is to effect changes in the way the West views the Orient, to direct the attention of Europeans and Americans to the appalling picture they have painted of this Eastern Other and thereby prompt its correction.

Said begins in the introduction by citing the principal assumptions which underlie his project. First, he argues that all knowledge is political, reflecting the desires and interests of those who formulate it. He strongly objects to "the general liberal consensus" that "pure" knowledge can be separated from political knowledge, or that knowledge can ever be impartial and objective.[11] "No one has ever devised a method for detaching the scholar from the circumstances of life, from the fact of his involvement (conscious or unconscious) with a class, a set of beliefs, a social position, or from the mere activity of being a member of society" (10).

Next, he delimits the range of his study: he will concentrate on the British, French, and American experience of the Near Orient—Islam and the Arab world—as this experience has developed since the end of the seventeenth century (16–17). He then asserts his assumption that no individual text on the Orient can be properly understood outside the body of all other Orientalist writings. This is because these texts borrow styles of description and evaluation from each other; they share concepts of this region of the world and its people. No text reproduces the "real" Orient, Said maintains, but rather all participate in a collective, Western vision of it (20–21).

Finally, he notes the "personal dimension" of *Orientalism.* He admits that he has more than a passing, scholarly interest in his subject. "Much of the personal investment in this study derives from my awareness of being an 'Oriental' as a child growing up in two British colonies" (25), Said announces. "The nexus of knowledge and power creating 'the Oriental' and in a sense obliterating him as a human being is therefore not for me an exclusively academic matter" (27).

What is most interesting about these premises for the student of literature is that Said makes little substantive distinction between literary and nonliterary texts. Throughout his book, he draws on all types of discourse, intermixing imaginative, scholarly, and other sorts of documents to illustrate and support his claim that the West has systematically debased the East. When he maintains that knowledge is politically saturated, he implies, as the chapters of his study attest, that literary as well as scholarly/factual knowledge is thoroughly political. When he claims that Orientalist texts borrow from each other, that none can be properly understood in isolation from the rest, he implies that literary works borrow from nonliterary ones, and vice versa, and that both types contribute to and should be interpreted in the context of Orientalist writings as a whole. In fact, in an important sense *all* discourses are literature for Said. Since his thesis is that the Western version of the Arab and Islamic world is nothing more than the politically motivated stories Westerners make up and tell about it, then so-called scholarly/factual texts as well as literary ones are, on Said's view, fictional creations, there being little difference between Oriental characters and settings created in a novel, poem, or short story and those manufactured in a history, sociological study, or speech by a politician.

Having stated the basic premises of his argument, Said opens the first chapter, "The Scope of Orientalism," with specific examples of Orientalist discourse. Evelyn Baring, Lord Cromer, who was England's representative in Egypt beginning in 1882, came out strongly against Egyptian nationalism in an essay that appeared in the *Edinburgh Review* in 1908. Cromer argued that the inhabitants of this Near Eastern British colony were incapable of self-rule and that it was best for them, even though they may not have understood or appreciated the fact, that their country be governed by England (36). "Subject races did not have it in them to know what was good for them" (37) was Cromer's attitude. Said further notes that in his two-volume *Modern Egypt,* Cromer records "a sort of personal canon of Orientalist wisdom" (38), consisting of such blatantly racist conclusions as the following:

> Orientals or Arabs are . . . gullible, "devoid of energy and initiative," much given to "fulsome flattery," intrigue, cunning, and unkindness to animals; Orientals cannot walk on either a road or a pavement (their disordered minds fail to understand what the clever European grasps immediately, that roads and pavements are made for walking); Orientals are inveterate liars, they are "lethargic and suspicious," and in everything oppose the clarity, directness, and nobility of the Anglo-Saxon race (38–39).

EDWARD W. SAID: POLITICAL CRITIQUE

Cromer contributes to what Said, in a 1976 interview, calls an "operative and effective knowledge by which he [the Oriental] was delivered textually to the West, occupied by the West, milked by the West for his resources, humanly quashed by the West."[12]

Said is quick to point out that Cromer's attitudes are not aberrations, that they are in fact fairly typical. What allows this British colonialist to say what he says is the existence of "a library or archive of information" about the Oriental that was "commonly and, in some of its aspects, unanimously held" (41). Literary artists also dipped into this archive to create their texts. "Even the most imaginative writers of an age," Said maintains, "men like [Gustave] Flaubert, [Gerard de] Nerval, or [Sir Walter] Scott, were constrained in what they could either experience or say about the Orient" (43). Said's repeated claim is that *every* Western observer of the East saw and recorded only what he or she had been conditioned by his or her culture to see and record. "Orientalism was ultimately a political vision of reality," he argues, "whose structure promoted the difference between the familiar (Europe, the West, "us") and the strange (the Orient, the East, "them")" (43). Novelists, poets, and playwrights participated in and advanced this vision just as did sociologists, historians, and statesmen.

In the second of the three lengthy chapters comprising *Orientalism,* Said traces the development of Orientalist discourse through a range of primarily nineteenth-century Western authors, including the anthropologist Silvestre de Sacy, the philologist Ernest Renan, and Flaubert. In his extended discussion of Flaubert, Said notes that the French author consistently depicts the Orient as a place of heightened lasciviousness and carnality. *Salambo,* for instance, is a novel which presents the Oriental woman as a fount of "luxuriant and seemingly unbounded sexuality" (187). Said maintains that in reducing Near Easterners to animal drives and instincts, "Flaubert was neither the first nor the most exaggerated instance of a remarkably persistent motif in Western attitudes to the Orient" (188). The idea that this region represents "not only fecundity but sexual promise (and threat), untiring sensuality, unlimited desire . . ." (188) was not Flaubert's creation. He perhaps gave this notion more "artistic dignity" than did other writers, but the idea itself is "singularly unvaried" in both literary and nonliterary accounts of the Arab world (188).

Said concludes his book with a chapter entitled "Orientalism Now" in which he demonstrates that the racist, demeaning, condescending attitudes present in Cromer, Flaubert, and their contemporaries and predecessors can also be found in more modern times. He notes that William Butler Yeats, in his 1930s poem "Sailing to Byzantium," repeats the widely held view of the Orient as an ancient civilization not subject to the changes and advances of history (230). He points out that in America, which since World War II has displaced France and Britain as the leader in world politics and thus as the principal site of Orientalist discourses, films and television consistently depict the Arab as lecherous, bloodthirsty, and dishonest: "He [the Arab] appears as an oversexed degenerate, capable, it is true, of cleverly devious intrigues, but essentially sadistic, treacherous, low" (286–87).

Kucich remarks that "Said's central argument about the discourse of Orientalism is that, despite significant shifts in strategy over the past two hundred years, it is essentially inca-

EDWARD W. SAID: POLITICAL CRITIQUE

pable of development. . . ."[13] The fiction of the Eastern Other, first created by Westerners centuries ago, has remained, Said believes, remarkably unchanged in its essential features up to the present.

Said does, however, find at least signs of hope for a more balanced, positive portrayal of the Orient in the work of such contemporary authors as Anwar Abdul Malek and Yves Lacoste (325). And he sees his own book as a caution against the "mind-forg'd manacles" created by Orientalist discourses (328). What he hopes for in the future, he insists in the book's final section, is not a more objectively accurate depiction of Arab reality. Echoing his beginning premise that all knowledge is political, he asserts: "It is not the thesis of this book to suggest that there is such a thing as a real or true Orient" (322). Because reality is always only what people perceive it to be through the filter of their cultural interests and values, then the "failures of Orientalism cannot be accounted for . . . by saying that the *real* Orient is different from Orientalist portraits of it. . ." (322). What Said believes in is the possibility of more flattering, less derogatory perceptions, in the West's ability to revise its politics so that it might create a new fiction replete with more favorable, humane images of the Oriental. It is for the production of such images that he urgently presses.

Critics have detected a tension, if not an outright contradiction, between Said's repeated premise that reality is necessarily constructed by the ways people interpret it and the claim, sometimes explicitly voiced and always implicit, that Orientalists present a false, skewed picture of the actual, factual Orient. How can Said at the same time suggest that Westerners have misrepresented the East to serve their political ends and that there is no "real or true Orient" to be represented, either in literary or nonliterary texts? "Said tells us that the Orient is always 'constituted'—the interpreter creates and produces it," William E. Cain points out. "Yet he repeatedly insists on the presence of Oriental 'reality' or 'realities,' implying that an Orient exists that is not the work of interpreters."[14] Cain's conclusion is that "there is an ambivalent relation between Said's commitment (he is an Arab Palestinian himself) to the manifestly 'real' people of the Orient, and his assumption that all areas of experience and knowledge are 'constituted.'"[15] The contradiction is never resolved; there are two distinct strands of thought in Said's work which never quite come together.

A related problem with the argument of *Orientalism* that has been raised is that if, as Said claims, people always create reality through already in-place discourses, then how is anyone, Said included, able to get outside those discourses in order to offer a critique of them? There is a real difficulty, Robert Young explains, in accounting for "how Said separates himself from the coercive structures of knowledge that he is describing."[16] The fabrication of less inflammatory, more positive images of the Arab that Said recommends implies an ability to transcend prevailing ways of perceiving the world, but Said never explains how exactly such transcendence is possible.

As real and profound as these problems are, they should not detract from the strength and importance of Said's work. "*Orientalism* is the product of an agile and powerful intelligence,"[17] Cain judges, despite his criticisms. The book, even with its unresolved tensions, leaves the reader with an exhaustive analysis of the way the Orient has been rendered in the West, a potent and largely convincing thesis about how cultural Others are created through the biases and self-interests of the home culture, and a timely challenge to avoid falling prey to demeaning stereotypes about alien societies. Because it represents one of the first serious and extended studies of imperialism, *Orientalism* "cannot be underestimated in its importance and in its effects," Young asserts. "Nor would it be overstating the case," he adds, "to say that much of the current pressure for the political [in criticism and theory], particularly in the U.S. where there is no recent substantial tradition of political criticism, has followed from the work [especially *Orientalism*] of Said."[18]

The World, the Text, and the Critic, a collection of fourteen essays written between 1969 and 1981, covers an array of topics that reiterate, deepen, and expand themes and concerns found in *Orientalism.* In "Introduction: Secular Criticism," Said identifies a current problem—from his 1970s perspective—with literary study and suggests a solution. The problem is that criticism has attempted to cut itself off from social and political concerns. "When our students are taught such things as 'the humanities,'" Said notes, "they are almost always taught that these classic texts embody, express, represent what is best in our, that is, the only, tradition. . . .[they are taught] that such fields as the humanities and such subfields as 'literature' exist in a relatively neutral political element. . . ."[19] Students are given little sense of how literary texts are shaped by and reflect the values and views of the specific cultures and historical periods that produced them. They are not made aware of the fact that there is more than one tradition and that "what is best in our[s]," its values and views, is not necessarily all good.

Equally problematic is the fad in advanced literary theory to retreat "into the labyrinth of 'textuality'" (3). Many contemporary critics, following the lead of such deconstructive luminaries as Jacques Derrida, treat texts as instances of pure, free-floating language, unencumbered by ties with real world economic, social, and political conditions. They devote their energies to detailing and accounting for the play of the text's words in isolation, analyzing "the aporias [unsolvable logical problems] and unthinkable paradoxes of a text" (4). Summing up his diagnosis of the current scene, Said asserts that "American or even European literary theory now explicitly accepts the principle of noninterference," refusing to concern itself with "anything that is worldly, circumstantial, or socially contaminated" (3).

In practice, this policy of noninterference simply does not work. Said's contention is that in the very act of divorcing itself from sociopolitical concerns, criticism plays a political and social role, namely, the maintenance of the state's in-place values, views, and policies. Avoiding the social and political dimension of texts, either by retreating to pure textuality or preaching the timeless "truths" of the Western classics, does not make the text's political and social commitments go away; rather, such avoidance simply means ignoring those commitments, leaving them intact, critically unchallenged. "[C]ontemporary criticism is an institution for publicly affirming the values of our, that is, European, dominant elite culture" (25), Said declares. The consequence of refusing to analyse the text's cultural affiliations "has been the regulated, not to say calculated, irrelevance of criticism, except as an adornment to what the powers of modern industrial society transact. . ." (25).

The solution to this problem, Said believes, is for criticism to engage the text more self-consciously in the worldly affairs it necessarily participates in, and further, to play an oppositional role in relation to any repressive or inhumane values and views such engagement might uncover. The critic, he concedes, is always intimately connected with his or her home culture: "the critical consciousness is part of its actual social world and of the literal body that the consciousness inhabits, not by any means an escape from either one or the other" (16). But connection does not have to take the form of complicity; it is possible for the critic to scrutinize and contest the state's power from a position within the confines of its documents. Critics may, in fact should, criticize objectionable, repressive attitudes that they find in texts, just as in *Orientalism* Said criticizes the image of the Near East that he discovers in his reading.

True criticism, Said maintains, is inherently oppositional. "Were I to use one word consistently along with *criticism,*" he asserts, "it would be *oppositional*" (29). The good critic is suspicious of "orthodox habits of mind," on the lookout for problems with accepted ways of representing the world (29). "For in the main," Said sums up the social mission of the critic, "criticism must think of itself as life-enhancing and constitutively opposed to every form of tyranny, domination, and abuse; its social goals are noncoercive knowledge produced in the interests of human freedom" (29).

Cain has criticized Said for vagueness, for recommending a very general "noncoercive knowledge," the particular details of which he never spells out.[20] John McGowan raises essentially the same concern that was broached in relation to *Orientalism.*

Though Said in this essay makes an attempt to account for how the critic can at one and the same time be a part of yet opposed to society, McGowan nonetheless detects an unresolved tension between these two strands in his thought. Furthermore, McGowan argues that there is a conflict between Said's implicit appeal to universal, transcendent notions of the good and his explicit assertion that all values are culturally relative, socially and historically conditioned. Said assumes that he can definitively, authoritatively say what is right and wrong about the views a text presents, yet he also maintains that concepts of rightness and wrongness vary in different societies and historical periods.[21]

The depths of Said's despair over the fact that too many critics in recent years have failed to engage sociohistorical issues in an oppositional way can clearly be felt in "Reflections on American 'Left' Literary Criticism." Those who advertise themselves most conspicuously as "oppositional" critics are often in truth, Said contends, most docilely complicit with state power. He is specifically referring here to the critical scene in the 1970s, primarily though not exclusively to deconstruction. In Said's own words, deconstructors and their like self-consciously adopt "a position of opposition to what is considered to be established or conservative academic scholarship," but their work, in the final analysis, does nothing more than "further solidify and guarantee the social structure and the culture that produced them" (159).

He cites Paul de Man as a prime offender. De Man shows "the impossibility of political and social responsibility" on the part of critics and poets (162). As Said reads him, this deconstructor argues that literature and its criticism are only about language,

EDWARD W. SAID: POLITICAL CRITIQUE

which is something entirely distinct from reality. Literature constitutes a closed universe of conventions and concepts that is removed from real world politics and social concerns; in commenting on texts, the critic is thus commenting only on this linguistic universe (162–64). In addition, de Man's method is fundamentally ironic, demonstrating that "when critics or poets believe themselves to be stating something, they are really revealing—critics unwittingly, poets wittingly—the impossible premises of stating anything at all. . ." (163). De Man, as noted in the first chapter of this book, argues that words have multiple, contradictory meanings; they do not communicate a single, stable message. This means, Said argues, that literature and criticism are incapable of making definitive truth claims of any sort, sociopolitical or otherwise. The de Manian critic is relegated to the politically irrelevant role of analyzing linguistic conundrums that the politically irrelevant poet formulates. De Man, Said concludes, elevates the literary work to "a position of almost unconditional superiority over historical facticity [reality] not by virtue of its power but by virtue of its admitted powerlessness. . ." (163). He plays straight into the hands of the cultural powers in that he deprives literature and its criticism of any potential to oppose those powers, to make a social difference.

After stirring even contemporary Marxists into the soup of leftist critics who have "succumbed to the passivity of ahistorical refinement upon what is already given, acceptable, and above all already defined" (168), Said reiterates points he earlier made in the introduction. Following Antonio Gramsci, an early twentieth-century Italian theorist, he calls for criticism that recognizes "art as belonging not to some free-floating ether or to some rigidly governed domain or iron determinism, but to some large intellectual endeavor—systems and currents of thought—connected in complex ways to doing things, to accomplishing certain things, to force, to social class and economic production, to diffusing ideas, values, and world pictures" (170). Critics should actively stand against social and political ills by oppositionally commenting upon literary texts, conceived of as such culturally engaged Gramscian documents. The critic's goals, Said concludes, should be "understanding, analyzing, and contending with the management of power and authority within the culture" (175).

In "Swift as Intellectual," the third chapter of *The World, the Text, and the Critic,* Said gives examples both of a socially engaged writer and socially engaged literary interpretation. Jonathan Swift has been unduly ignored by contemporary critics, Said contends, partly because of the way he has been interpreted in the past by commentators such as George Orwell, who views him as "reactionary, nihilistic, and diseased"; as a political conservative who lacks faith in the common man (76). Said dissents, arguing that Orwell "is not so much wrong as characteristically partial, insufficient, not really political enough in his verdict" (76). Said believes that Swift is a keen critic of social ills of his time who should not be criticized, as Orwell implicitly does, for lacking a twentieth-century mentality.

More specifically, Said argues that one of the reasons Orwell rejects Swift's political and social vision is because Swift does not come down squarely on the side of representative democracy (77). That is, Swift does not promote the idea that people are capable of policing themselves, that everyone should be given an equal voice in the construction and governance of society. Said points out, however, that it is unfair to censure Swift for this shortcoming since the modern notion of representative democracy was not current in the eighteenth century. Swift cannot be denounced for failing to espouse a position that his culture did not make available. "Swift is very much a part of his time," says Said, "there is no point therefore in expecting him to think and act like a prototype of George Orwell since the cultural options, the social possibilities, the political activities offered Swift in his time were more likely to produce a Swift than an Orwell" (77).

Without in any way endorsing Swift's conservative side, Said asserts that one should concentrate credit on what Orwell himself admits is prominent in Swift: a steadfast opposition to the particular social and political tyrannies—"spy trials, informers, police plots, and so on"—that Swift found operative in his world. "Orwell seems unable to realize," remarks Said, "that one can be steadfastly opposed to tyranny, as Swift was all his life, and not have a well-developed position on 'representative institutions'" (77). In Said's judgment, Swift was a self-conscious, worldly intellectual who powerfully and effectively attacked specific injustices and abuses of power prevalent in his age.

Said avoids the problem of critical worldlessness, of which he is so censorious throughout *The World, the Text, and the Critic,* in several ways. First, he identifies a writer who is openly concerned with sociopolitical issues and then focuses upon those issues. Second, he reads these concerns with a social and political eye. He places Swift historically and culturally, seeing his views not as universal and absolute truths but as ideas conditioned by and responding to the specific circumstances of his day. He then passes politically charged judgments on Swift, championing in the eighteenth century writer the political position—opposition to tyranny—which he as a twentieth-century, Western democratic thinker finds appealing and correct. Finally, he interprets Orwell oppositionally, refusing simply to accept Orwell's interpretation of Swift, criticizing instead those aspects of Orwell's analysis that he thinks are mistaken and diminish Swift's contributions.

Said's recent book, *Culture and Imperialism,* broadens and complicates the concerns of *Orientalism* and *The World, the Text, and the Critic.* In the opening paragraph, Said places his text in relation to *Orientalism,* observing that in the present study "I . . . have tried. . . to expand the argument of the earlier book [*Orientalism*]."[22] Michael Gorra remarks that *Culture and Imperialism* is perhaps not "a conceptual breakthrough on the same order as 'Orientalism'" and that "very little" of it is "absolutely fresh."[23] Nonetheless, Gorra is highly complimentary of the book—he refers to its "usefulness" and "importance," calls it "urgently needed"[24]—a judgment more than justified by Said's demonstrated ability to take old themes in new directions and to extend implications of previous arguments in ways which add significantly to his earlier work.

Said's thesis is that nineteenth- and twentieth-century Britain, France, and America cannot be properly understood outside the context of imperialism; he explicitly refers to imperialism as "the major . . . determining, political horizon of modern Western culture" (60). The logic of imperialism, introduced earlier in *Orientalism* and amplified here, is grounded in notions of conquest and exploitation, dominance and submission. Western colonialists, past and present, see themselves as wholly other than the non-Westerners they colonize. "There is an 'us' and a 'them,'" Said observes, "each quite settled, clear, unassailably self-evident" (xxv). The "them" are deemed by the "us" to be "lesser peoples, with lesser rights, morals, claims" (36) and are thus consigned to "a secondary racial, cultural, ontological status" (59). According to imperialist logic, it is up to the colonizers—it is their duty in fact—to rule those whose lands they invade: "there was virtual unanimity [among the colonizers] that subject races should be ruled, that they *are* subject races, that one race deserves and has consistently earned the right to be considered the race whose main mission is to expand beyond its own domain" (53).

Europeans in the nineteenth and early part of the twentieth century rarely entertained the idea that the desires and needs of those they conquered should be heeded. Notes Said, "there is only infrequently an acknowledgment that the colonized people should be heard from, their ideas known" (50).

Much of the first half of *Culture and Imperialism* is devoted to showing how imperialism and its crushing logic are woven into the fabric of nineteenth- and twentieth-century British and French literary texts. For instance, the second section of the second chapter concentrates on references to the British Empire in Jane Austen's *Mansfield Park*. The lord of Mansfield Park, Sir Thomas Bertram, sustains his estate through profits from property he owns in Antigua, a British colony in the Caribbean: "according to Austen we are to conclude that no matter how isolated and insulated the English place (e.g., Mansfield Park), it requires overseas sustenance" (89). Said further points out that though only passing references are made to these foreign possessions, such holdings being so common at the time that Austen does not feel the need to feature them, the reader is led to believe that Bertram owns a sugar plantation, a typical colonialist enterprise in Antigua, one which entailed merciless exploitation of the slaves and their land (89). These references to empire, Said declares, "are not dead historical facts but, as Austen certainly knew, evident historical realities" (89). Austen's fictional allusions to British overseas interests reflect their real, if taken for granted, historical importance.

More telling than references to colonial holdings themselves, Said believes, are structures of thought and behavior depicted in the novel that, without ever explicitly being tied to Antigua, reflect the colonialist mentality. For instance, he points to a passage in which Bertram magisterially, dictatorially sets his Mansfield house in order. Said argues that "Sir Thomas does exactly the same things—on a larger scale—in his Antigua 'plantations'" (87). The way this man runs his household in England is the way he manages his foreign property, namely, by assuming a superior position of command and discipline over his subjects. The logics governing the control of these two separate spheres—an English manor and a colonial plantation—infect and connect each other.

Said also notes ways in which Fanny Price, the eventual "spiritual mistress" (84) of Mansfield, evidences colonialist structures of consciousness through attitudes that, on the surface, have nothing whatsoever to do with the British Empire. At one point Fanny is overwhelmed by the small, cramped quarters she finds at Portsmouth, her home before moving to Mansfield Park.

EDWARD W. SAID: POLITICAL CRITIQUE

"In too small a space," Said registers her realization, "you cannot see clearly, you cannot think clearly, you cannot have regulation or attention of the proper sort" (88). Fanny's need for expanded space, Said contends, mirrors and metaphorically justifies the British urge to conquer other lands in order to fulfill its supposed destiny. Just as Fanny cannot be a full and vital person in quarters that are too cramped, Austen implies, so Britain cannot be a full and vital nation in such circumstances (88–89).

This imperialist logic ingrained in literary texts such as *Mansfield Park* and endemic to Western culture as a whole is subject to Said's constant attack. He praises modern African writers who in various ways have resisted geographical and cultural colonization by white Westerners and insisted on repossessing their native lands and traditions (209–20). He undermines the imperialist "us"/"them" mentality by arguing that national and racial identities are neither wholly distinct nor fixed and constant; rather, they are hybrid formations, always capable of rearrangement and reformulation. "Partly because of empire," Said maintains, "all cultures are involved in one another; none is single and pure, all are hybrid, heterogenous, extraordinarily differentiated, and unmonolithic" (xxv). To see nations and races as interconnected is to move away from structures of dominance and submission and toward tolerance and empathy. If people's identities are all so meshed, then to abuse the other is, implicitly, to abuse oneself. By learning to view cultures as inescapably linked with each other, societies, Said hopes, can begin to "formulate an alternative" to the "destructive politics of confrontation and hostility" (18).

In the final chapter of his book, "Freedom from Domination

in the Future," Said extends his call for an anti-imperialist tomorrow. After a lengthy analysis of contemporary American imperialist ventures—stressing the recent war with Iraq—he finalizes the suggestion, which he has made throughout his book, that we move beyond colonialist ways of looking at the world. He hopefully notes "the demystification of all cultural constructs, 'ours' as well as 'theirs,'" which has been carried out in recent years by such scholars as Hayden White, Fredric Jameson, Foucault, and Derrida (304). These progressive intellectuals demonstrate that divisions between nations and races are not ordained by nature, but manufactured by people.

Repeating points he has made earlier, Said maintains that a first step in dismantling imperialism is to see different cultures' fates and identities as intimately connected with each other (311–12). He recommends Paul Virilio's model of "counter-habitation." We must learn to assume the attitude of migrants and exiles, never identifying too strongly with "our" group, constantly exploring and inhabiting the "other" (331–32). "Survival in fact is about the connections between things," (336) Said declares. Finding such connections will allow for "a collective human existence . . . not based on coercion or domination" (335). Said closes his book with the following prescriptive admonition: It is more rewarding—and more difficult—to think concretely and sympathetically, contrapuntally, about others than only about 'us.' But this also means not trying to rule others, not trying to classify them or put them in hierarchies, above all, not constantly reiterating how 'our' culture or country is number one (or *not* number one, for that matter). For the intellectual there is quite enough of value to do without *that* (336).

EDWARD W. SAID: POLITICAL CRITIQUE

There is at least some truth in John Leonard's charge that Said "repeats himself ad infinitum throughout the book."[25] *Culture and Imperialism* might be condensed; Said does tend to rehash the same points, probably because the book's chapters are based upon individual, self-contained lectures originally delivered in 1985–86 (xi). However, the points he makes are all interesting, provocative, and useful, and each rehash does to some degree add to earlier points, providing further details or casting previous claims in a different light. Said's analysis of imperialism is a significant contribution to the themes and concerns he has focussed upon throughout his career.

CHAPTER SEVEN

Richard Rorty
Neopragmatism

Richard Rorty was born in October 1931 in New York City, New York. He received his B.A. from the University of Chicago in 1949, his M.A. from Yale University in 1952, and his Ph.D. from Yale in 1956. Before joining the faculty at the University of Virginia in 1982, where he is presently Kenan Professor of Humanities, he taught philosophy at Wellesley College (1958–61) and Princeton University (1961–82). Among his many honors are a Guggenheim fellowship, 1973–74, and a MacArthur Prize fellowship, 1981–86.[1] Rorty has edited two important collections of philosophical papers, *The Linguistic Turn: Recent Essays in Philosophical Method* (1967) and *Philosophy in History: Essays in Philosophic Method* (1992). In addition to publishing essays in leading journals, he has written five major books: *Philosophy and the Mirror of Nature* (1979), *Consequences of Pragmatism: Essays 1972–1980* (1982), *Contingency, Irony, and Solidarity* (1989), *Essays on Heidegger and Others* (*Philosophical Papers* vol. I, 1991), and *Objectivity, Relativism, and Truth* (*Philosophical Papers,* vol. 2, 1991).

Rorty is a pragmatist philosopher. One of his chief models and a thinker often cited in his work is John Dewey, likely the most important figure in the history of American pragmatism. Truth, Rorty holds, is not to be equated with accurate depiction of reality. It is not that which the mind directly discovers in the world outside itself. Rorty rejects the idea that consciousness mirrors, either by exactly reproducing or selectively focussing, objective facts. Circumventing all forms of representationalism—theories of how reality is reflected in consciousness—Rorty argues for an instrumentalist, use-value version of knowledge. Truth is practice, not reflection. It is that which people in particular societies at particular times find to be helpful and valuable in living their lives. It is beliefs and actions that contribute to achieving culturally and historically relative goals.

Rorty maintains that since the only world human beings can ever have or know is the one they construct through their conceptual frameworks, their ways of looking at things, then any attempt to discover or focus objective facts is a useless exercise. What does or does not count as a fact cannot be determined by scrutinizing reality as it is in itself, but is instead decided by the terms in which people, motivated by their needs and desires, choose to conceive of the world. Rather than wasting time worrying about how things *really* are, the pragmatist concerns him or herself with how people make things to serve their ends.

For instance, Rorty's pragmatist would not seek to define gender by referring to facts of nature. What does it mean to be a woman? The pragmatist answer would be that it means what people decide it should mean. Femininity is not an objectively existing set of traits to be discovered. Rather, descriptions of the feminine are made up by individuals in society in order to serve their purposes. The "fact" of what women are or are not is manufactured by the terms in which women are conceptualized instead of being built into the fabric of reality. To say, for

example, that a woman's primary role is to raise children and
provide emotional support for her husband is, on Rorty's view,
neither accurately nor inaccurately to reflect objective facts of
nature; it is instead merely to identify characteristics that people
in a particular culture at a particular time—America in the 1950s,
for instance—ascribe to women in order to assure that society
functions as they wish. This definition of femininity has been
challenged and, to a significant degree, changed in recent years
because cultural goals, values, and structures of power have
changed, not because people now have a clearer vision of the
eternal essence of womanhood, what women "really" are, than
they did in the past.

As Richard Shusterman has observed, Rorty "is probably the
most influential contemporary American philosopher on literary
theory."[2] Throughout his work, Rorty opposes literary ways of
knowing the world to forms of knowledge developed in traditional philosophy, making it clear that he prefers the former,
which is wholly consistent with the pragmatist perspective, to the
latter, which is not. Literature and literary criticism, he believes,
are more useful tools for coping with and understanding the
world than traditional philosophy has been. Most of Rorty's
heroes are literary critics and theorists or poets and novelists.
Many of the philosophers he treats in detail—such figures as
Immanuel Kant, Friedrich Nietzsche, and Martin Heidegger—
are important and often cited in literary/critical circles.

Rorty's informal, witty style—he is prone to such colorful
formulations as "societies or literary texts are [not] squishier than
molecules"[3] and "pragmatists think that one will suffer from
Hume's itch only if one has been scratching oneself with what has

sometimes been called 'Hume's fork.' . . ."[4]—makes his work palatable and appealing to literary critics who might shy away from the often turgid, arcane, and highly technical language of mainstream professional philosophers.

Philosophy and the Mirror of Nature, Rorty's first major book, is one of the most influential and widely read philosophical studies to have appeared in recent memory. Cornel West calls it "a landmark text, the most important book in American metaphilosophy [philosophy about other works of philosophy] since Dewey's *The Quest for Certainty* (1929). . . ."[5] Likewise, the first sentence of Richard J. Bernstein's 1980 review announces: "Richard Rorty has written one of the most important and challenging books to be published by an American philosopher in the past few decades."[6] And in a 1981 review, Ian Hacking notes that Rorty's study "is causing numerous young people to read philosophical classics as never before. This is the closest thing to a cult book commencing popular philosophy that we have seen for many a year."[7]

Rorty here lays out the pragmatist argument, summed up above, which will serve as the basis for all his work. His emphases and articulations in this first book differ in certain respects from those in the later ones, but the core message remains the same. *Philosophy and the Mirror of Nature* is an evaluative history of philosophy, an interpretation of the Western tradition from a pragmatist perspective with detailed suggestions about the direction in which philosophy should proceed in the future. In the first half of his study, Rorty critically surveys pre-twentieth-century philosophy, concentrating on such central figures as René Descartes, John Locke, and Kant. He identifies and attempts to dissolve the mind-as-mirror-of-nature metaphor that he finds present everywhere. As Shusterman puts it, Rorty's attack is directed against the "traditional idea and ideal of knowledge as faithful representation of reality, where the mind is compared to a mirror that reflects the real and where philosophy's central task is . . . testing and repairing the mirror so that the propositions we assert will reflect the given realities with greater accuracy."[8] Rorty then focuses on the claims of certain contemporary philosophers—Wilfrid Sellars, W. V. O. Quine, T. S. Kuhn—who, he thinks, are on the correct, pragmatist track. For the most part, though not entirely, he seconds their claims, thereby laying the groundwork for his own position.

In the final chapter, Rorty sets forth in detail his belief that the type of knowledge literature yields is truer, which is to say more useful, than that produced by traditional philosophy. He expresses this belief through a distinction between what he labels systematic and edifying philosophy. Systematic philosophers are the mainstream thinkers he identifies in the first half of his book— Descartes, Locke, and Kant. These philosophers "are constructive and offer arguments"; they "build for eternity"; they seek *the* truth.[9] Knowledge, they think, is about the essential, fundamental structure of objective reality as it is perceived by the mind. Systematic philosophers spend their time constructing elaborate models that are meant accurately to picture the eternal nature of things. Edifying philosophers, on the other hand, recognize that truth is different for different people in different cultures in different historical periods. These thinkers, such peripheral figures as William James, John Dewey, Ludwig Wittgenstein, and Martin Heidegger, know that knowledge is, as

RICHARD RORTY: NEOPRAGMATISM

Rorty defines it early in his book, "what we are justified in believing," justification being "a social phenomenon rather than a transaction between 'the knowing subject' and 'reality'" (9). They know that what is true is simply what people in communities decide to make true in order to achieve their ends. The edifying philosopher is aware that "this century's 'superstition' was the last century's triumph of reason . . . that the latest scientific achievement, may not express privileged representations of essences, but be just another of the potential infinity of vocabularies in which the world can be described" (367). He or she subscribes to Rorty's conviction that, as West puts it, "ideas, words, and language are not mirrors which copy the 'real' or 'objective' world but rather tools with which we cope with 'our' world."[10]

Freed from the need to discover *the* truth, edifying philosophers, Rorty's heroes, pursue invention. Theirs is "the 'poetic' activity of thinking up . . . new aims, new words, or new disciplines. . ." (360). They are "literary" in that they strive, like the poet and the novelist, to create interesting and original ways of looking at the world, to persuade others that "what we are justified in believing" can be something fresh and different from what we believed in the past. "Edifying philosophers want to keep space open for the sense of wonder which poets can sometimes cause—wonder that there is something new under the sun, something which is *not* an accurate representation of what was already there. . ." (370). As West points out, Rorty shares with Ralph Waldo Emerson the conviction that "poetic activity constitute[s] the most noble of human practices."[11]

Rorty extends the concept of literature to cover not only

those texts that have traditionally been labelled literary—novels, plays, poems, short stories—but also other sorts of works, such as certain philosophical treatises, that forego the systematic, scientific search for absolute truth in favor of creative, useful interpretations of experience. As a matter of fact, he implies that even nonliterary, scientific texts are, from the pragmatist perspective, literary in the sense that all they really provide are man-made descriptions of the world, despite their pretensions to be yielding objective facts. The nonliterary text is simply a literary text whose language reflects a deluded belief in the possibility of discovering *the* truth.

Philosophy and the Mirror of Nature may be read as a work of literary theory and criticism because it offers a definition of literature which carefully distinguishes the literary from the nonliterary attitude and provides analyses of texts that fit this definition. Rorty maintains that "the point of edifying philosophy is to keep the conversation going rather than to find objective truth" (377). The course of knowledge, he holds, should be viewed as analogous to a conversation: voices play off of and respond to each other, progressing as they will. Edifying philosophers, like literary artists, promote this view, seeing knowledge in these terms and sounding new voices that extend their culture's talk. This is the direction which Rorty recommends that philosophy proceed in the future. Philosophers should give up the vain task of seeking *the* truth and become, in Rorty's sense of the word, poets, actively participating in their culture's ever-changing conversation of ideas.

More than half of the thirteen essays in Rorty's next book, *Consequences of Pragmatism,* were written during or before the year *Philosophy and the Mirror of Nature* was published. The rest, excluding the introduction, had appeared by 1980. As Christopher W. Gowans points out, the major themes of the first book are also the themes of the second, but in *Consequences of Pragmatism* "these themes . . . are given more succinct formulations through an examination of more diverse and broader contexts."[12] Some of these contexts include the philosophies of Wittgenstein and Stanley Cavell, fictional discourse, irrationalism, professional philosophy, and the social sciences. Giles Gunn claims that "no small amount" of contemporary literary criticism has been "influenced by the position Rorty takes so powerfully in *Consequences of Pragmatism*."[13] It is in such influential essays as "Philosophy as a Kind of Writing: An Essay on Derrida" and "Nineteenth-Century Idealism and Twentieth-Century Textualism" that Rorty helps carve out the currently popular view of culture as a collection of interconnected texts whose relationships and meanings can be "infinitely redescribed."[14] These two essays, along with the lengthy and well-known introduction, will be the focus of the discussion that follows.

"Introduction: Pragmatism and Philosophy" is another attempt to distinguish the literary from the nonliterary and to promote the former while redefining its traditional boundaries. Rorty begins this essay by recommending that we stop doing Philosophy and do philosophy. Philosophy with a capital "P" is traditional philosophy, the systematic sort associated with Descartes, Locke, and Kant in *Philosophy and the Mirror of Nature*. Capital "P" Philosophy looks for *the* truth, attempts properly to picture how thought or language hooks up with, reflects, objective reality in a once-and-for- all fashion. Philosophy with a small "p," on the other hand, is the pragmatist project

Rorty earlier announced. The small "p" philosopher is not out to provide new, truer answers to age-old Philosophical questions about the nature of reality, but rather to give interesting, useful descriptions of things in particular social and historical settings.[15] While the Philosopher labors to show that ideas and practices are effective and make sense because they are true, the philosopher demonstrates that to show an idea or practice to be effective and to make sense is just the same thing as to show it is true (xxix). What makes sense and is effective, and thus what is true, is nothing more nor less than what helps people "cope with their environment," accomplish the goals they set for themselves (xviii).

Small "p" philosophy is, for Rorty, synonymous with literature. He suggests that those works which advance the pragmatist version of truth, whether they be the sort traditionally classified as literature or those commonly called philosophy, are literary, while those that purport to tell *the* truth are nonliterary. Toward the end of his essay, Rorty evokes C. P. Snow's notions of literary and scientific cultures, endorsing the goal of the former, which is simply to think up interesting and useful ways of conceptualizing experience, and renouncing the aim of the latter, which is to discover eternal truths (xli). Rorty believes that if science would drop its universalizing and absolutizing pretensions, it would be just "one genre of literature" (xliii). He thinks that those participating in Snow's scientific culture are engaged in a quixotic enterprise; science does not, as the scientist believes, discover the ultimate nature of reality but rather is simply one way among many of talking about the human experience of the material world, a way no more nor less true than other forms of talking such as novels, poems, or plays.

Criticisms have been levied against the pragmatist stance Rorty takes in the introduction to *Consequences of Pragmatism* as well as in the rest of his works. One common objection, registered by commentators such as Christopher Norris, is that if what is true is merely that which constitutes an interesting and useful way of conceptualizing experience, then it is not possible to judge as objectively, factually false a view which the majority in a particular society deems to be interesting and useful. But surely such judgments are sometimes in order.[16] If, for example, people accept as true an idea that science later proves to be false—for instance that the earth is flat rather than round—then this idea, Rorty's critics would argue, must be false, in the present world as in the past, despite the fact that it was deemed interesting and useful, and thus true, in the society in which it was formulated. Rorty is, Norris argues, an "ultra-relativist" who is stuck in the untenable position of maintaining that the validity of a poet's or philosopher's vision of things is strictly a matter of public opinion and taste.[17]

In "Philosophy as a Kind of Writing: An Essay on Derrida," the sixth chapter in *Consequences of Pragmatism,* Rorty enlists the progenitor of deconstruction as an ally in his pragmatist cause. Derrida accurately understands, Rorty believes, that texts are finally only about themselves; they express only the meanings their words convey, and do not refer to a set of objective facts outside language. The Kantian tradition, which Derrida opposes, "thinks of truth as a vertical relationship between representations and what is represented," a hooking up of language with reality (92). The French philosopher belongs to an alternate tradition, grounded in the thought of the nineteenth-century German phi-losopher G. W. F. Hegel, which "thinks of truth horizontally—as the culminating reinterpretation of our predecessors' reinterpre-tations of their predecessors' reinterpretations. . ." (92). For Derrida, to philosophize is to discover hidden meanings in words rather than in reality. Truth and knowledge are textual in that they are stated in and derived from language. The innovative philoso-pher is the one who interprets existing ways of describing the world in fresh and interesting terms (94–96).

Derrida's starting point is "the wish to revolt against the eternalization and cosmologization of the present vocabulary by creating a new vocabulary. . ." (103). Every formulation of reality, he shows, can be undermined—deconstructed—to create a new and different formulation. Rorty strongly endorses Derrida's conclusion that "no one can make sense of the notion of a last commentary, a last discussion note, a good piece of writing which is more than the occasion for a better piece" (109). The French deconstructionist's position is consistent with the American pragmatist's view that all descriptions of the world are man-made, the products of particular imaginations in particular his-torical and cultural circumstances, always subject to change and revision.

Derrida's emphasis, which Rorty wholeheartedly affirms, on the textual basis of truth and knowledge is echoed and expanded in "Nineteenth-Century Idealism and Twentieth-Cen-tury Textualism." Here Rorty traces the lineage of textualism, placing it in a pragmatist line that descends from certain philoso-phers from the previous century. Prior to Hegel, Rorty argues, the history of philosophy was the story of various efforts to explain

RICHARD RORTY: NEOPRAGMATISM

how the mind mirrors the eternal truths of objective reality. It was the scientific project of discovering the one, true description of things (143–46). Hegel, whose major texts appeared in the early part of the nineteenth century, switched directions by asserting that the truths of reality change as people's ways of looking at reality change. His was a "literary" philosophy in so far as it insisted upon "the historical sense of the relativity of principles and vocabularies to a place and time, the romantic sense that everything can be changed by talking in new terms. . ." (149). Hegel's vision, however, proved to be only partially, not wholly, literary.

Early in "Nineteenth-Century Idealism and Twentieth-Century Textualism," Rorty declares that a key feature of "what I shall call 'literature'" is that "it succeeds simply by its success, not because there are good reasons why poems or novels or essays should be written in the new way rather than the old" (142). By "good reasons" he means justification in terms of proximity to absolute, final truth. Rorty is saying that literary artists do not alter descriptions of reality in order to get closer to such truth, but rather they alter them simply to produce fresher, more interesting and useful ways of looking at the present world. Put another way, they are pragmatist philosophers; in this essay, as in the first one in the book, he equates literature with pragmatism. Rorty's argument is that Hegel was not a full-fledged literary/pragmatist thinker because he held that descriptions of reality evolve through time as man's consciousness evolves. Ultimate reality, Hegel believed, is Absolute Spirit—the mind of God—which man's thought progressively unfolds and reveals in historical stages (147–50). Though Hegel's philosophy was literary, in Rorty's sense of the term, insofar as it recognized that reality changes as talk about reality changes, it was not literary in that these changes were conceived of as stages in a predetermined course toward some ultimate, final goal.

It was Friedrich Nietzsche and William James, toward the end of the century, who recognized that the Hegelian model was, in fact, not literary enough. They completed the pragmatist turn, each in his own terms, by arguing that though it was certainly the case that reality alters as descriptions of it alter, new descriptions "help get us what we want" rather than, as Hegel postulated, bring us closer to *the* truth (150). The views James and Nietzsche developed are "the philosophical counterpart of literary modernism, the kind of literature which prides itself on its autonomy and novelty rather than its truthfulness to experience or its discovery of pre-existing significance" (153). It is in this pragmatist literary camp that Rorty situates Derrida and other strong textualists such as the contemporary theorists and philosophers Michel Foucault and Harold Bloom, who see the search for truth as nothing more than the process of creatively reinterpreting already existing interpretations of the world.

"I think we shall best understand the role of textualism within our culture," Rorty concludes, "if we see it as an attempt to think through a thorough-going pragmatism, a thorough-going abandonment of the notion of *discovering the truth* which is common to theology and science" (150–51). Like Nietzsche and James, the contemporary textualist knows that talk about the world can never truly be science, even if it sometimes deludedly presents itself as such, but is always literature, which makes and remakes reality rather than discovers its objective essence.

RICHARD RORTY: NEOPRAGMATISM

Rorty's pragmatism is put to work in his next book, *Contingency, Irony, and Solidarity,* to "suggest the possibility of a liberal utopia."[18] He begins by repeating the central thesis of all his work: reality is made by the ways people think and talk, not found in a set of objective facts. The "liberal utopia" he envisions is a world in which each individual pursues his or her personal constructions of reality without infringing upon the rights and abilities of others to pursue theirs. On the one hand, people in this society are concerned with the welfare of the community at large in that they take care to respect and nourish the needs and desires of their neighbors, while on the other hand they are extremely self-centered in that everyone focuses upon formulating and fulfilling his or her personal projects. "The closest we will come to joining these two quests [for self-creation and human solidarity]," Rorty sums up his position, "is to see the aim of a just and free society as letting its citizens be as privatistic, 'irrationalist,' and aestheticist as they please so long as they do it on their own time—causing no harm to others and using no resources needed by those less advantaged" (xiv).

The ideal citizen of this "liberal utopia," the individual who most effectively pursues his or her personal projects without interfering with the rights of others, is a "liberal ironist." At the beginning of chapter four, "Private Irony and Liberal Hope," Rorty describes the ironic attitude in detail, squarely positioning it against the urge to discover absolute truth. Ironists are pragmatists who reject the idea that there is only one authentic way to see and talk about the self and its environment. In Rorty's terminology, the ironist dispenses with "final vocabularies," viewing each statement of the way things are as just one of many such statements and as an invitation to generate yet others (73). He or she is what Rorty, borrowing from the French philosopher Jean-Paul Sartre, calls "'meta-stable'"; the self exists as a constant potential for different self-actualizations, as a propensity to interpret reality in a variety of ways (73–74). Such individuals are "never quite able to take themselves seriously because [they are] always aware that the terms in which they describe themselves are subject to change, always aware of the contingency and fragility of their final vocabularies, and thus of their selves" (73–74). Rorty sees self-creation as, ideally, an ongoing, revisionary process, not as something one does once and stops, content that final truth has been attained.

Throughout his book, Rorty associates pragmatic self-creation with literature. Another name for the liberal ironist is "poet," which for Rorty includes literary artists, critics, theorists, unorthodox philosophers, and all others who think of reality as made rather than found and who attempt to describe themselves and their worlds in fresh and original terms. Rorty devotes much of *Contingency, Irony, and Solidarity* to giving examples of and praising those who have championed and achieved this poetic stance. He applauds Nietzsche's revolutionary urging that individuals write and rewrite their personal scripts, that they compose their lives as highly original poems. "To fail as a poet—and thus, for Nietzsche, to fail as a human being," Rorty approvingly pronounces, "is to accept somebody else's description of oneself, to execute a previously prepared program, to write, at most, elegant variations on previously written poems" (28). Marcel Proust's unique aptitude for fashioning the self through idiosyncratic reactions to the particulars—people, places, experiences—

of his specific existence is also singled out by Rorty for approval. Proust's autobiographical novel, *Remembrance of Things Past,* is "a network of small, interanimating contingencies" which represents its author's imaginative, poetic construction of his personal story, securing for him a sense of what Rorty most prizes, "[p]rivate autonomy" (100–101).

Also important to Rorty is Harold Bloom, whose "strong poet" fights the fear "that one might end one's days in . . . a world one never made, an inherited world" (29). The strong poet, whether he or she be an author of verse, a philosopher, a literary critic, or some other type of writer, is capable of rebelling against the influences of others to fashion his or her own, unique voice (29). Nietzsche, Proust, and Bloom are, like all ironists, literary thinkers who unlike traditional philosophers and scientists know that truth is not built into the world to be read out of it but is rather manufactured by creative acts of interpretation (78–80).

Though self-creation is his principal focus, Rorty also discusses community at length. His notion of the ideal society is simple. Echoing ideas from the introduction, he proclaims in "The Contingency of a Liberal Community," that "J. S. Mill's suggestion that governments devote themselves to optimizing the balance between leaving people's private lives alone and preventing suffering seems to me pretty much the last word" (63). The "liberal" in "liberal ironist" signifies this attitude of hesitating to intervene in the lives of others except in order to deter injustice and pain. Rorty endorses Judith Shklar's definition, formulated in her 1984 book *Ordinary Vices,* of the "liberal" as one who "believes that cruelty is the worst thing we do" (146). The way to diminish cruelty, he maintains, is to enlarge the scope of what Wilfrid Sellars refers to as "'we intentions'" (190). By extending "our sense of 'we' to people whom we have previously thought of as 'they,'" we increase our capacity for sympathy and thereby decrease the likelihood of misusing others (192). Sounding a great deal like Said in *Culture and Imperialism,* Rorty maintains that people are much less apt to be cruel to one of "us" than to one of "them." Social solidarity, as earlier noted, means respecting the idiosyncratic, poetic quests for self-actualization that others are embarked upon.

There is certainly the possibility of conflict between pursuit of one's personal, poetic program and respect for others' projects. One might well act cruelly toward one's neighbor in order to actualize one's private self. Rorty treats this problem in detail in chapter seven of his book, "The Barber of Kasbeam: Nabokov on Cruelty." In such texts as *Pale Fire* and *Lolita,* contemporary Russian-American novelist Vladimir Nabokov depicts characters whose self-absorption leads them to ignore the rights and feelings of their fellows. As Rorty reads them, these novels are their author's warning against the dangers inherent in the ironist's quest to construct him or herself exactly as he or she pleases. "[S]uch books show how our attempts at autonomy, our private obsessions with the achievement of a certain sort of perfection, may make us oblivious to the pain and humiliation we are causing. They are the books which dramatize the conflict between duties to self and duties to others" (141). The implicit lesson of this chapter is that one must carefully balance one's personal ambitions against the larger good of the community. Nabakov's literary, poetic texts serve as a critique of the literary, poetic attitude taken to a certain extreme.

RICHARD RORTY: NEOPRAGMATISM

There is a problem, Richard Arneson believes, with Rorty's concept of cruelty: it is entirely too vague. Rorty defines cruelty as "the infliction of unnecessary or disproportionate suffering," yet he "disdains to give any account at all that would help identify when the point of necessity or due proportion has been reached."[19] Furthermore, Gunn maintains that Rorty tends to oversimplify and sometimes distort the positions of those philosophers and artists he cites in *Contingency, Irony, and Solidarity,* as he does in his other works.[20] Despite these and other criticisms, *Contingency, Irony, and Solidarity* is, as Stephen K. White puts it, "a remarkable book," one which impressively advances its author's pragmatist cause.[21]

On the premises of his own view, Rorty must concede to his critics that his claims are subject to attack. As he states early in his book, "anything can be made to look good or bad by being redescribed" (73). He knows that his texts, like anyone else's, can legitimately be construed from perspectives that highlight deficiencies in their arguments. Rorty's position provides for, even encourages, its own dismantling and revision, its own poetic, pragmatic interpretation.

Rorty's recent books, *Philosophical Papers: Objectivity, Relativism, and Truth* (Volume I) and *Essays on Heidegger and Others* (Volume II), continue ideas that were introduced in *Philosophy and the Mirror of Nature* and extend through *Contingency, Irony, and Solidarity*. There are no radical departures here, not surprisingly since the essays comprising these two texts were actually written during or before the time his second and third books appeared. Though many of the figures and issues he addresses are different, the pragmatist perspective, articulated in fresh tones and with new twists, remains the same. Just how closely connected the latest books are with the earlier ones is reflected in Richard T. Vann's observation that the two volumes "although not intended as an introduction to his [Rorty's] positions, serve that purpose quite well."[22] William I. Buscemi goes so far as to intersperse citations from *Contingency, Irony, and Solidarity* with references to the *Philosophical Papers* in his essay review of the latter, demonstrating clearly and concretely the overlap between earlier and later texts.[23]

A single essay from the second volume will suffice to illustrate Rorty's treatment of familiar themes in these most recent books. In "Heidegger, Kundera, and Dickens," Rorty once again asserts his preference for literary, as opposed to philosophical, knowledge. Philosophers attempt to discover the eternal essence of reality, to give the one accurate account of things. He cites the influential twentieth-century thinker Martin Heidegger as an example. Heidegger's strategy, like that of all traditional philosophers, is to sum up the essential premises and assumptions of Western thought, identify what is false about those premises and assumptions, and then assert his own version of ultimate, absolute truth.[24] Using him for somewhat different purposes than he did in *Philosophy and the Mirror of Nature,* Rorty contends that Heidegger turns out to be just another version of the "ascetic priest, the person who wants to set himself apart from his fellow humans by making contact with what he calls his 'true self' or 'Being' or 'Brahma' or 'Nothingness'" (71). Rorty concedes that such seekers after the Absolute are "very *useful* people" (72). In rejecting past accounts of "objective" reality and presenting new ones, they cause "cultures to change themselves, to break out of a tradition into a previously unimagined future" (73). What he rejects is these seekers' conviction that the changes they recommend mark progress toward understanding the way things *really* are. Each new philosophical view, as Rorty sees it, is in actuality just another man-made description of the world, a fresh way of creating reality rather than a more accurate reflection of it.

As useful as philosophy is, Rorty favors the novel as a medium for understanding the world. It is the novelist, not the philosopher, who gives us the best, most enlightened descriptions. Drawing on remarks made by the contemporary novelist Milan Kundera, Rorty maintains that this fictional form presents reality as it actually is: a multiplicity of voices and perspectives, a human construct rather than a set of objective facts. For the philosopher's insistence on getting things right, the novelist substitutes "a display of diversity of viewpoints, a plurality of descriptions of the same event" (74). Novels promote the creation of what Rorty conceives of as an ideal world: "a paradise of individuals in which everybody has the right to be understood but nobody has the right to rule" (75). Such a paradise, he argues, will be possible only when people stop imagining, as does the philosopher, that a single person or group can define the way things are for everyone, and start realizing, as does the novelist, that truth is just what different people make it.

Rorty singles out Charles Dickens as a model novelist. Dickens's genius lies in presenting a panoply of distinct individuals. Observes Rorty, "the most celebrated and memorable feature of his novels is the unsubsumable, uncategorizable idiosyncrasy of the characters" (78). Rather than standing for general, abstract truths and principles, his creations are wholly themselves, unique and inimitable: "the names of Dickens's characters *take the place* of moral principles and of lists of virtues and vices. They do so by permitting us to describe each other as 'a Skimpole,' 'a Mr. Pickwick,' 'a Gradgrind,' 'a Mrs. Jellyby,' 'a Florence Dombey'" (78). Dickens's pictures of people do "an enormous amount for equality and freedom" in that they foster an appreciation for the diversity of human pursuits and perspectives (79). His novels, Rorty concludes, increase the reader's "ability to be comfortable with a variety of different sorts of people" and thereby contribute to the possibility of a world in which everyone is willing "to leave people alone to follow their own lights" (81). In short, Dickens is a pragmatist, a poet who produces original and useful descriptions of things, implicitly renouncing the drive to discover the one, final truth.

The sixth essay, "Inquiry as Recontextualization: An Anti-Dualist Account of Interpretation," in Part I of *Objectivity, Relativism, and Truth,* opens with the following instruction to the reader:

Think of human minds as webs of beliefs and desires, of sentential attitudes—webs which continually reweave themselves so as to accommodate new sentential attitudes. Do not ask where the new beliefs and desires come from. Forget for the moment about the external world, as well as about that dubious interface between self and world called "perceptual experience." Just assume that new ones keep popping up and that some of them put strains on old beliefs and desires.[25]

RICHARD RORTY: NEOPRAGMATISM

This passage sums up as neatly as any the general attitudes Rorty repeatedly assumes. The search for truth is not about discovery of the way things *really* are. It is about understanding "webs of beliefs and desires." The question of how these webs connect with the "external world" is irrelevant. Rorty brackets out—forgets—objective reality, concerning himself solely with "sentential attitudes," the ways people judge the world to be. Beliefs and desires are not fixed and constant but rather change and develop. New ones "keep popping up," placing "strains on old beliefs and desires." Truth alters, reality is transformed, as the fabric of man-made ideas is continually rewoven in poetic, literary acts of creation. This, in a nutshell, is the neopragmatist position that Rorty develops throughout his work.

NOTES

Chapter 1: Introduction

1. Leitch, *American Literary Criticism From the Thirties to the Eighties,* 9.

2. Ibid., 8–9.

3. Ibid., 11–14.

4. Robey, "Anglo-American New Criticism," 65.

5. Ibid.

6. Ibid., 72–83, and Leitch, *American Literary Criticism,* 24–35.

7. Leitch, *American Literary Criticism,* 62.

8. Ibid., 60–61.

9. Ibid., 63.

10. Ibid., 64–65.

11. Corman, "Chicago Critics," 144–45.

12. Leitch, *American Literary Criticism,* 80.

13. Frye, *Anatomy of Criticism,* 6.

14. Eagleton, *Literary Theory,* 92.

15. Leitch, *American Literary Criticism,* 238.

16. Eagleton, *Literary Theory,* 96–97.

17. Barthes, "The Structuralist Activity," 172.

18. Ibid.

19. Ibid.

20. Eagleton, *Literary Theory,* 105.

21. Leitch, *American Literary Criticism,* 248–49.

22. Spikes, "Present Absence Versus Absent Presence," 333.

23. Ibid., 334–36.

24. Ibid., 338.

25. Ibid.

26. Leitch, *American Literary Criticism,* 267–68.

27. Poster, "Foucault," 277.

28. Ibid. 278.
29. E. D. Hirsch, *Validity in Interpretation,* 48.
30. Ibid., 50.
31. Ibid., 8.
32. Fish, *Is There a Text in This Class?,* 310.
33. Ibid., 320.
34. Ibid., 305–6.
35. Bloom, *The Anxiety of Influence,* 5.
35. Ibid., 70.
37. de Bolla, *Harold Bloom,* 18–20.
38. Bloom, *The Anxiety of Influence,* 95.
39. Hartman, *Criticism in the Wilderness,* 53.

Chapter 2: Paul de Man

1. Dekane, "de Man, Paul (Adolph Michael) 1919–1983," 111.
2. Lehman, *Signs of the Times,* 143.
3. Ibid.
4. Ibid., 143–44, 154.
5. "Yale Scholar's Articles Found in Nazi Paper," 1.
6. Lehman, *Signs of the Times,* 163–65.
7. Ibid., 166.
8. Ibid., 269–71.
9. Moynihan, "Interview with Paul de Man," 584.
10. Sophocles, *Oedipus,* l. 73.
11. Moynihan, "Interview," 587.
12. Ibid., 580.
13. Bate, "The Crisis in English Studies," 195–212.
14. Abrams, "The Deconstructive Angel," 425–38.
15. Moynihan, "Interview," 586.
16. Lentricchia, *After the New Criticism,* 284.

17. Ray, *Literary Meaning,* 188.
18. de Man, *Blindness and Insight,* vii; hereafter cited in the text.
19. Norris, *Deconstruction,* 22.
20. Brooks, "The Language of Paradox," 34.
21. Hirsch, *The Deconstruction of Literature,* 136.
22. Culler, "Paul de Man," 81.
23. de Man, *Allegories of Reading,* ix; hereafter cited in the text.
24. Selden, *A Reader's Guide to Contemporary Literary Theory,* 94.
25. Chase, "De Man, Paul," 196.
26. Norris, *Paul de Man,* xii.

Chapter 3: Henry Louis Gates, Jr.

1. "Gates, Henry Louis, Jr., 1950–," 154.
2. Bloom, Review of *Loose Canons,* 21.
3. Ward, "An Interview with Henry Louis Gates, Jr.," 928.
4. Gates, *Figures in Black,* ix–xi; hereafter cited in the text.
5. Werner, "Recent Books on Modern Black Fiction," 126.
6. Wideman, "Playing, Not Joking, With Language," 3.
7. Mason, Review of *The Signifying Monkey,* 1681.
8. Gates, *The Signifying Monkey,* 4; hereafter cited in the text.
9. Olney, "Henry Louis Gates, Jr.," 132.
10. Warren, Review of *The Signifying Monkey,* 225.
11. Gates, *Loose Canons,* xv; hereafter cited in the text.
12. "Separate but Equal," 105.
13. Bloom, Review of *Loose Canons,* 21.

Chapter 4: Elaine Showalter

1. "Showalter, Elaine 1941–," 524.
2. Fraiman, "An Interview with Elaine Showalter," 16.

3. Ibid.
4. "Showalter, Elaine 1941–," 524.
5. Showalter, "Feminist Criticism in the Wilderness," 184.
6. Ibid., 184–85.
7. Ibid., 186.
8. Ibid., 197.
9. Ibid., 201.
10. Fraiman, "Interview," 9.
11. Ibid., 10.
12. Jackson, "Women of Doubtful Gender," 67.
13. Showalter, *A Literature of Their Own,* 11; hereafter cited in the text.
14. Fraiman, Interview, 9.
15. Jackson, "Women of Doubtful Gender," 70.
16. Krause, Review of *A Literature of Their Own,* 217.
17. Ferguson, "Women's Literature," 314.
18. Fraiman, "Interview," 10.
19. Showalter, *The Female Malady,* 5; hereafter cited in the text.
20. Spacks, "'Crazy Ladies?'" 36.
21. Karp, Review of *The Female Malady,* 1427.
22. Showalter, *Sexual Anarchy,* 3; hereafter cited in the text.
23. Smith-Rosenberg, Review of *Sexual Anarchy,* 546.
24. Baym, Review of *Sister's Choice,* 629.
25. Showalter, *Sister's Choice,* 2; hereafter cited in the text.
26. Showalter, Introduction to *Daughters of Decadence,* vii.
27. Ibid., viii.

Chapter 5: Stephen Greenblatt

1. "Greenblatt, Stephen Jay 1943–," 225.
2. Selden, *Contemporary Literary Theory,* 103–5.
3. Ibid., 104.

4. Greenblatt, *Renaissance Self-Fashioning,* 3; hereafter cited in the text.

5. King, Review of *Renaissance Self-Fashioning,* 184.

6. Ibid.

7. Mullaney, Review of *Shakespearean Negotiations,* 499.

8. Ibid., 496.

9. Greenblatt, *Shakespearean Negotiations,* 23; hereafter cited in the text.

10. Norbrook, Review of *Shakespearean Negotiations,* 117.

11. Greenblatt, *Learning to Curse,* 1; hereafter cited in the text.

12. Eagleton, Review of *Learning to Curse,* 7.

13. Veeser, "Introduction," xi.

14. Schama, "They All Laughed at Christopher Columbus," 30.

15. Greenblatt, *Marvelous Possessions,* 12; hereafter cited in the text.

16. Echevarría, "Europeans in Wonderland," 22.

Chapter 6: Edward W. Said

1. "Said, Edward W. 1935–," 759.

2. Sprinker, "Introduction," 2.

3. "Said, Edward W. 1935–," 759.

4. Sprinker, "Introduction," 2.

5. Salusinszky, Interview with Edward Said, 128.

6. Ibid., 138.

7. Wicke and Sprinker, "Interview with Edward Said," 249.

8. Said, *Beginnings,* 18–19; hereafter cited in the text.

9. Morris, Review of *Beginnings,* 738.

10. Kucich, "Edward W. Said," 253.

11. Said, *Orientalism,* 10; hereafter cited in the text.

12. "Interview/Edward Said," 41.

13. Kucich, "Edward W. Said," 253.

14. Cain, Review of *Orientalism,* 212.

15. Ibid., 212–13.

16. Young, *White Mythologies,* 127.

17. Cain, Review of *Orientalism,* 210.

18. Young, *White Mythologies,* 126.

19. Said, *The World, the Text, and the Critic,* 21; hereafter cited in the text.

20. Cain, "Criticism and Knowledge," 184.

21. McGowan, *Postmodernism and Its Critics,* 165–67.

22. Said, *Culture and Imperialism,* xi.

23. Gorra, "Who Paid the Bills at Mansfield Park?" 11.

24. Ibid.

25. Leonard, "Novel Colonies," 383.

Chapter 7: Richard Rorty

1. "Rorty, Richard 1941–," 428.

2. Shusterman, "Rorty, Richard," 626.

3. Rorty, *Objectivity, Relativism, and Truth,* 40.

4. Ibid.

5. West, *The American Evasion of Philosophy,* 199.

6. Bernstein, "Philosophy in the Conversation of Mankind," 745.

7. Hacking, "A Rebirth of Philosophy?" 33.

8. Shusterman, "Rorty, Richard," 626.

9. Rorty, *Philosophy and the Mirror of Nature,* 369; hereafter cited in the text.

10. West, *The American Evasion of Philosophy,* 201.

11. Ibid., 204.

12. Gowans, "Intuition and Argument in Philosophy," 133.

13. Gunn, *Thinking Across the American Grain,* 96.

14. Ibid.

15. Rorty, *Consequences of Pragmatism,* xvi; hereafter cited in the text.

16. Norris, *Uncritical Theory,* 126–27.

17. Ibid, 127.

18. Richard Rorty, *Contingency, Irony, and Solidarity,* xv; hereafter cited in the text.

19. Arneson, Review of *Contingency, Irony, and Solidarity,* 478.

20. Gunn, *Thinking Across the American Grain,* 99–100.

21. White, Review of *Contingency, Irony, and Solidarity,* 690.

22. Vann, Review of *Philosophical Papers,* 1173.

23. Buscemi, "The Ironic Politics of Richard Rorty," 141–54.

24. Rorty, *Essays on Heidegger and Others,* 68–71.

25. Rorty, *Objectivity, Relativism, and Truth,* 93.

BIBLIOGRAPHY

History of Contemporary Theory

Barthes, Roland. "The Structuralist Activity." In *Contemporary Literary Criticism: Literary and Cultural Studies,* 2d ed. Edited by Robert Con Davis and Ronald Schleifer, 169–74. New York: Longman, 1989. Barthes introduces principles of structuralism.

Bloom, Harold. *The Anxiety of Influence: A Theory of Poetics.* New York: Oxford University Press, 1973. Bloom argues that new texts are produced through oedipal struggles with old texts.

Corman, Brian. "Chicago Critics." In *The Johns Hopkins Guide to Literary Theory and Criticism,* edited by Michael Groden and Martin Kreiswirth, 143–45. Baltimore: Johns Hopkins University Press, 1994. Corman gives an overview of the Chicago school, identifying central assumptions and principal figures.

de Bolla, Peter. *Harold Bloom: Towards Historical Rhetorics.* New York: Routledge, 1988. De Bolla focuses upon Bloom's notion of rhetoric, explaining and attempting to extend it.

Eagleton, Terry. *Literary Theory: An Introduction.* Minneapolis: University of Minnesota Press, 1983. Eagleton outlines and critiques, from a marxist perspective, major schools of thought in twentieth-century literary theory.

Fish, Stanley. *Is There a Text in This Class? The Authority of Interpretive Communities.* Cambridge, MA: Harvard University Press, 1980. Fish presents his view that the meaning of a text is constituted by the reader.

Frye, Northrop. *Anatomy of Criticism.* Princeton: Princeton University Press, 1957. Frye classifies literary texts and figures in terms of modes, symbols, myths, and genres.

Hartman, Geoffrey H. *Criticism in the Wilderness: The Study of Literature Today.* New Haven: Yale University Press, 1980. Hartman reviews the current state of criticism and examines the relationship between literature and criticism.

Hirsch, E. D., Jr. *Validity in Interpretation.* New Haven: Yale University Press, 1967. Hirsch argues that a literary text's meaning is fixed and stable, though its significance may vary from interpreter to interpreter.

Leitch, Vincent B. *American Literary Criticism From the Thirties to the Eighties.* New York: Columbia University Press, 1988. Leitch outlines central premises of and identifies major figures in twentieth-century American literary criticism and theory.

Poster, Mark. "Foucault, Michel." In *The Johns Hopkins Guide to Literary Theory and Criticism,* edited by Michael Groden and Martin Kreiswirth, 277–80. Baltimore: Johns Hopkins University Press, 1994. Poster gives an overview of Foucault's central assumptions and major texts.

Robey, David. "Anglo-American New Criticism." In *Modern Literary Theory: A Comparative Introduction,* edited by Ann Jefferson and David Robey, 65–83. Totowa, N.J.: Barnes and Noble, 1982. Robey identifies principal New Critics, traces the development of the New Criticism, and identifies this movement's central assumptions.

Spikes, Michael P. "Present Absence Versus Absent Presence: Kripke Contra Derrida." *Soundings* 75 (1992): 333–55. Spikes summarizes Derrida's position, criticizes it, and then offers alternatives grounded in the language philosophy of Saul Kripke.

Paul de Man

Primary Works de Man, Paul.

de Man, Paul. *Aesthetic Ideology,* edited by Andrzej Warminski. Minneapolis: University of Minnesota Press, 1988.

———. *Allegories of Reading: Figural Language in Rousseau, Nietzsche, Rilke, and Proust.* New Haven: Yale University Press, 1979.

———. *Blindness and Insight: Essays in the Rhetoric of Contemporary Criticism.* 2d ed. Minneapolis: University of Minnesota Press, 1979.

———. *Critical Writings: 1953–1978,* edited by Lindsay Waters. Minneapolis: University of Minnesota Press, 1989.

———. *The Resistance to Theory.* Minneapolis: University of Minnesota Press, 1986.

———. *The Rhetoric of Romanticism.* New York: Columbia University Press, 1984.

———. *Romanticism and Contemporary Criticism: The Gauss Seminars and Other Papers,* edited by E. S. Burt, Kevin Newmark, and Andrzej Warminski. Baltimore: Johns Hopkins University Press, 1992.

———. *Wartime Journalism, 1940–1942.* Edited by Werner Hamacher, Neil Hertz, and Tom Keenan. Lincoln, NE: University of Nebraska Press, 1989.

Interview

Moynihan, Robert. "Interview with Paul de Man." *Yale Review* 73 (1984): 576–602.

Secondary Sources

Abrams, M. H. "The Deconstructive Angel." *Critical Inquiry* 3 (1977): 425–38. Abrams criticizes deconstruction, arguing against the notion that meaning is radically indeterminate.

Bate, Walter Jackson. "The Crisis in English Studies." *Scholarly Publishing,* 14 April 1983, 195–212. Bate attacks deconstruction, maintaining that texts communicate clear, unequivocal meaning and values.

BIBLIOGRAPHY

Brooks, Cleanth. "The Language of Paradox." In *Contemporary Literary Criticism: Literary and Cultural Studies,* 2d ed. Edited by Robert Con Davis and Ronald Schleifer, 33–42. New York: Longman, 1989. Brooks argues that poems unify discordant ideas into organic wholes.

Chase, Cynthia. "De Man, Paul." In *The Johns Hopkins Guide to Literary Theory and Criticism,* edited by Michael Groden and Martin Kreiswirth, 194–97. Baltimore: Johns Hopkins University Press, 1994. Chase surveys de Man's career, identifying his central arguments and summarizing his principal works.

Culler, Jonathan. "Paul de Man." In *Dictionary of Literary Biography: Modern American Critics Since 1955,* vol. 67, 74–89. Detroit: Bruccoli Clark/Gale Research, 1988. Culler provides biographical information about de Man and summarizes the central arguments of his books and essays.

DeKane, Carol Lynn. "de Man, Paul (Adolph Michael) 1919–83." In *Contemporary Authors,* edited by Susan M. Trosky, vol. 128, 111–13. Detroit: Gale Research, 1990.

Hamacher, Werner, Neil Hertz, and Thomas Keenan, eds. *Responses On Paul de Man's Wartime Journalism.* Lincoln, Nebr.: University of Nebraska Press, 1989. Werner, Hertz, and Keenan collect essays by notable contemporary critics who comment on the relationship between de Man's youthful Nazi writings and his mature literary theory and criticism.

Hirsch, David H. *The Deconstruction of Literature: Criticism After Auschwitz.* Hanover, NH: Brown University Press, 1991. Hirsch criticizes de Man's mature literary theory as a retrospective effort to cover past Nazi sympathies.

Lehman, David. *Signs of the Times: Deconstruction and the Fall of Paul de Man.* New York: Poseidon Press, 1991. Lehman criticizes deconstruction in general, provides details about de Man's life, relates those details to the theorist's mature views, and points out problems with those views.

BIBLIOGRAPHY

Lentricchia, Frank. *After the New Criticism*. Chicago: University of Chicago Press, 1980. Lentricchia's book, which describes and evaluates major theoretical schools of thought in the twentieth-century, contains a lengthy discussion of de Man, focussing upon the theorist's neglect of the role history and culture play in the production of literary meaning.

Norris, Christopher. *Deconstruction: Theory and Practice*. London: Methuen, 1982. Norris provides a general introduction to deconstruction, which contains a summation of de Man's theory.

————. *Paul de Man: Deconstruction and the Critique of Aesthetic Ideology*. New York: Routledge, 1988. Norris surveys de Man's work, tracing the development of his thought and focussing upon his criticism of the notion that literature can directly communicate lived experience.

Ray, William. *Literary Meaning: From Phenomenology to Deconstruction*. Oxford: Basil Blackwell, 1984. One of the chapters in Ray's book provides an introduction to de Man's thought.

Selden, Raman. *A Reader's Guide to Contemporary Literary Theory*. 2d ed. Lexington, Ky.: University Press of Kentucky, 1989. Selden provides a brief, elementary introduction to de Man's theory.

"Yale Scholar's Articles Found in Nazi Paper," *New York Times,* 1 December 1987, sec. 2, p. 1. This article announces and details the discovery of pro-Nazi articles that de Man wrote in his youth for Belgian publications.

Henry Louis Gates, Jr.

Primary Works

Gates, Henry Louis, Jr. *The Amistad Chronology of African-American History, 1990*. New York: Amistad, 1993.

BIBLIOGRAPHY

——. *Colored People*. New York: Knopf, 1993.

——. *Figures in Black: Words, Signs, and the Racial" Self*. New York: Oxford University Press, 1987.

——. *Loose Canons: Notes on the Culture Wars*. New York: Oxford University Press, 1992.

——. *The Signifying Monkey: A Theory of African-American Literary Criticism*. New York: Oxford University Press, 1988.

——, ed. *Bearing Witness: Selections from African-American Autobiography in the Twentieth Century*. New York: Pantheon, 1991.

——, ed. *Black Literature and Literary Theory*. New York: Routledge, Chapman, and Hall, 1984.

——, ed. *The Classic Slave Narratives*. New York: Dutton, 1987.

——, ed. *In the House of Oshubgo: Critical Essays on Wole Soyinka*. New York: Oxford Univesity Press, 1985.

——, ed. *Our Nig*. By Harriet E. Wilson. New York: Vintage, 1983.

——, ed. *"Race," Writing, and Difference*. Chicago: University of Chicago Press, 1986.

——, ed. *Reading Black, Reading Feminist: A Critical Anthology*. New York: Dutton, 1990.

——, ed. *The Schomburg Library of Nineteenth-Century Black Women Writers*. New York: Oxford University Press, 1988.

Gates, Henry Louis, Jr., and K. A. Appiah, eds. *Alice Walker: Critical Perspectives Past and Present*. New York: Amistad, 1993.

——, eds. *The Dictionary of Global Culture*. New York: Knopf, 1995.

——, eds. *Gloria Naylor: Critical Perspectives Past and Present*. New York: Amistad, 1993.

——, eds. *Langston Hughes: Critical Perspectives Past and Present*. New York: Amistad, 1993.

——, eds. *Richard Wright: Critical Perspectives Past and Present*. New York: Amistad, 1993.

——, eds. *Toni Morrison: Critical Perspectives Past and Present*. New York: Amistad, 1993.

BIBLIOGRAPHY

————, eds. *Zora Neale Hurston: Critical Perspectives Past and Present.* New York: Amistad, 1993.

Gates, Henry Louis, Jr. and George Houston Bass, eds. *Mule Bone: a Comedy of Negro Life.* By Langston Hughes and Zora Neale Hurston. New York: Harper Perennial, 1991.

Gates, Henry Louis, Jr. and Charles T. Davis, eds. *Black Is the Color of the Cosmos: Charles T. Davis's Essays on Black Literature and Culture.* New York: Garland, 1982.

————, eds. *The Slave's Narrative: Texts and Contexts.* New York: Oxford University Press, 1983.

————, et al., eds. *Speaking of Race, Speaking of Sex: Hate Speech, Civil Rights, and Civil Liberties.* New York: New York University Press, 1994.

Interview

Ward, Jerry W., Jr.. "Interview with Henry Louis Gates, Jr." *New Literary History* 22 (1991): 927–35.

Secondary Sources

Bloom, James D., review of *Loose Canons,* by Henry Louis Gates, Jr. *New York Times Book Review,* 9 August 1992, 21. Bloom sees *Loose Canons* as its author's call for all Americans, black and white, to study African American literature, since black writers have played a central role in shaping American culture as a whole.

"Gates, Henry Louis, Jr. 1950–." In *Contemporary Authors: New Series,* edited by Hal May and Deborah A. Straub, vol. 25, p. 154. Detroit: Gale Research, 1989.

Mason, T. O., review of *The Signifying Monkey,* by Henry Louis Gates, Jr. *Choice* 26 (1989): 1681. Mason asserts that *The Signifying Monkey* is an essential, indispensable text for all students of African American literature.

Olney, James. "Henry Louis Gates, Jr." In *Dictionary of Literary Biography: Modern American Critics Since 1955,* vol. 67, 129–33. Detroit: Bruccoli Clark/Gale Research, 1988. Olney provides biographical information about Gates and surveys his major texts through *The Signifying Monkey,* summing up their principal theses.

"Separate but Equal." Review of *Loose Canons,* by Henry Louis Gates, Jr. *Economist,* 27 June 1992, 105. The reviewer criticizes Gates for promoting a segregationist stance, for arguing that black literature and its criticism should be considered apart from white literature and its criticism.

Warren, Kenneth, review of *The Signifying Monkey,* by Henry Louis Gates, Jr. *Modern Philology* 88 (1990): 224–26. Warren reads Gates's book as an application of Harold Bloom's theory of influence to the black literary tradition.

Werner, Craig. "Recent Books on Modern Black Fiction: An Essay Review." *Modern Fiction Studies* 34 (1988): 125–35. Werner defends Gates against the charge that his work, particularly *The Signifying Monkey,* ignores the social and political dimension of black texts by focusing on their purely literary qualities.

Wideman, John, "Playing, Not Joking, With Language," review of *The Signifying Monkey,* by Henry Louis Gates, Jr. *New York Times Book Review,* 14 August 1988, 3. Wideman applauds Gates for his original interpretations of specific black texts and for developing a concept—signifying—that allows the reader to see how black texts are interconnected with and play off of each other in creative ways.

Elaine Showalter

Primary Works

Showalter, Elaine. *The Female Malady: Women, Madness, and English Culture, 1830–1980.* New York: Pantheon Books, 1985.

BIBLIOGRAPHY

———. "Feminist Criticism in the Wilderness." *Critical Inquiry* 8 (1981): 243–70.

———. "Introduction." In *Daughters of Decadence: Women Writers of the Fin-de-Siecle,* edited by Elaine Showalter. New Brunswick, N.J.: Rutgers University Press, 1993.

———. *A Literature of Their Own: British Women Novelists From Bronte to Lessing.* Princeton: Princeton University Press, 1977.

———. *Sexual Anarchy: Gender and Culture at the Fin de Siecle.* New York: Viking, 1990.

———. *Sister's Choice: Tradition and Change in American Women's Writing.* Oxford: Clarendon, 1991.

———, ed. *Alternative Alcott.* New Brunswick, NJ: Rutgers University Press, 1988.

———, ed. *Little Women.* By Louisa May Alcott. New York: Penguin, 1989.

———, ed. *The New Feminist Criticism: Essays on Women, Literature, and Theory.* New York: Pantheon, 1985.

———, ed. *Speaking of Gender.* New York: Routledge, 1988.

———, ed. *These Modern Women: Autobiographical Essays from the Twenties,* 2d ed. New York: Feminist Press, 1988.

———, ed. *Women's Liberation and Literature.* New York: Harcourt, 1971.

———, Lea Baechler, and A. Walton Litz, eds. *Modern American Women Writers.* New York: Collier Books, 1993.

Interview

Fraiman, Susan. "An Interview with Elaine Showalter." *Critical Texts: A Review of Theory and Criticism,* 4 (1987): 7–17.

Secondary Sources

Baym, Nina, review of *Sister's Choice,* by Elaine Showalter, *American Literature* 64 (1992): 629–30. Baym sees quilting—the piecing

BIBLIOGRAPHY

together of bits of material into an artistic pattern—as the central metaphor for women's writing that Showalter exploits throughout her book.

Ferguson, Maira, "Women's Literature: The Continuing Debate,"review of *A Literature of Their Own*, by Elaine Showalter, *Prairie Schooner* 51 (1977): 313–14. Ferguson criticizes Showalter for affirming certain traditionally masculine ways of looking at women's literature.

Jackson, Rosemary, "Women of Doubtful Gender: Sexual Politics and the Novel," review of *A Literature of Their Own*, by Elaine Showalter, *Encounter* 49 (1977): 67–77. Jackson praises Showalter's book for its originality, singling out for special commendation its vision of the female literary tradition as dynamic and evolving.

Karp, H., review of *The Female Malady*, by Elaine Showalter, *Choice* 23 (1986): 1427. Karp praises Showalter for expertly demonstrating that ideas about women in psychiatry reflect the particular historical and cultural circumstances that produced those ideas.

Krause, Agate Nesaule, review of *A Literature of Their Own*, by Elaine Showalter, *Criticism* 20 (1978): 216–18. Krause generally praises *A Literature of Their Own*, though she is critical of Showalter's failure to engage the political dimension of Virginia Woolf's work.

"Showalter, Elaine 1941–." In *Contemporary Authors*, edited by Cynthia R. Fadool, vols. 57–60, 524. Detroit: Gale Research, 1976.

Smith-Rosenberg, Carroll, review of *Sexual Anarchy*, by Elaine Showalter, *American Historical Review* 97 (1992): 545–46. Smith-Rosenberg sees *Sexual Anarchy* as a book about boundary crossings between such separate domains as politics and the physical body, history and literature, and masculinity and femininity.

BIBLIOGRAPHY

Spacks, Patricia Meyer, "Crazy Ladies?," review of *The Female Malady,* by Elaine Showalter, *New Republic,* 28 April 1986, 34–36. Spacks criticizes Showalter for reducing female mental illnesses to purely social and cultural causes.

Stephen Greenblatt

Primary Works

Greenblatt, Stephen. *Learning to Curse: Essays in Early Modern Culture.* New York: Routledge, 1990.

———. *Marvelous Possessions: The Wonder of the New World.* Chicago: University of Chicago Press, 1991.

———. *Renaissance Self-Fashioning: From More to Shakespeare.* Chicago: University of Chicago Press, 1980.

———. *Shakespearean Negotiations: The Circulation of Social Energy in Renaissance England.* Berkeley, Calif.: University of California Press, 1988.

———. *Sir Walter Ralegh: The Renaissance Man and His Roles.* New Haven: Yale University Press, 1973.

———. *Three Modern Satirists: Waugh, Orwell, and Huxley.* New Haven: Yale University Press, 1965.

———, ed. *Allegory and Representation: Selected Papers from the English Institute, 1979–80.* Baltimore: Johns Hopkins University Press, 1988.

———, ed. *Identifying Histories: Eastern Europe Before and After 1989.* Berkeley, Calif.: University of California Press, 1995.

———, ed. *The New World: Essays in Memory of Michel de Certeau.* Berkeley, Calif.: University of California Press, 1991.

———, ed. *New World Encounters.* Berkeley, Calif.: University of California Press, 1993.

BIBLIOGRAPHY

————, ed. *The Power of Forms in the English Renaissance.* Norman,
Okla.: Pilgrim Press, 1982.

————, ed. *Representing the English Renaissance.* Berkeley, Calif.
University of California Press, 1987.

Greenblatt, Stephen and Giles Gunn, eds. *Redrawing the Boundaries:
The Transformation of English and American Literary Studies.* New
York: Modern Language Association of America, 1992.

Secondary Sources

Eagleton, Terry, review of *Learning to Curse,* by Stephen Greenblatt,
Times Literary Supplement, 18 January 1991, 7. Eagleton praises
Greenblatt for seeing works of art as shaping as well as being shaped
by their historical and cultural contexts.

Echevarría, Roberto González, "Europeans in Wonderland," review of
Marvelous Possessions, by Stephen Greenblatt, *New York Times
Book Review,* 16 February 1992, 22–23. Echevarría criticizes
Greenblatt for presenting random, largely disconnected commentar-
ies on the exploitation of the New World by Europeans.

"Greenblatt, Stephen Jay 1943–." In *Contemporary Authors,* edited by
Claire D. Kinsman, vols. 49–52, 225. Detroit: Gale Research, 1975.

King, John N., review of *Renaissance Self-Fashioning,* by Stephen
Greenblatt, *Modern Philology* 80 (1982): 183–85. King argues that
the essays comprising Greenblatt's book can be read as separate, self-
contained units, though the essays collectively constitute a general
overview of sixteenth-century attitudes.

Mullaney, Steven, review of *Shakespearean Negotiations,* by Stephen
Greenblatt, *Shakespeare Quarterly* 40 (1989): 495–500. Mullaney
applauds *Shakespearean Negotiations* for expertly detailing the
complex interconnections between particular plays by Shakepeare
and the historical and cultural contexts in which they were written.

Norbrook, David, review of *Shakespearean Negotiations,* by Stephen

BIBLIOGRAPHY

Greenblatt, *Review of English Studies* 41 (1990): 116–18. Norbrook criticizes Greenblatt for overlooking the distinctive elements of Shakespeare's art in an effort to situate his plays in their cultural contexts.

Schama, Simon, "They All Laughed at Christopher Columbus," review of *Marvelous Possessions,* by Stephen Greenblatt, *New Republic,* 6 January 1992, 30–40. Schama compliments Greenblatt for expertly detailing the relationship between natives and invaders in the New World.

Selden, Raman. *A Reader's Guide to Contemporary Literary Theory,* 2d ed. Lexington, Ky.: University Press of Kentucky, 1989. Selden gives a brief, simplified description of the new historicism and Greenblatt's place in it.

Veeser, H. Aram. "Introduction." In *The New Historicism,* edited by H. Aram Veeser. New York: Routledge, 1989: ix–xvi. Veeser provides an advanced introduction to the New Historicism and notes Greenblatt's contributions.

Edward W. Said

Primary Works

Said, Edward W. *After the Last Sky: Palestinian Lives.* New York: Pantheon Books, 1986.

————. *Arabs and Jews:* Possibility of Concord. North Dartmouth, Mass.: Association of Arab-American University Graduates, 1974.

————. *Beginnings: Intention and Method.* New York: Columbia University Press, 1975.

————. *Covering Islam: How the Media and the Experts Determine How We See the Rest of the World.* New York: Pantheon Books, 1981.

BIBLIOGRAPHY

———. *Culture and Imperialism.* New York: Knopf, 1993.

———. *Identity, Authority, and Freedom: The Potentate and the Traveller.* Cape Town: University of Cape Town Press, 1991.

———. *Joseph Conrad and the Fiction of Autobiography.* Cambridge, MA: Harvard University Press, 1966.

———. *Musical Elaborations.* New York: Columbia University Press, 1991.

———. *Nationalism, Colonialism, and Literature: Yeats and Decolonization.* Derry: Field Day, 1988.

———. *Orientalism.* New York: Vintage, 1979.

———. *The Palestine Question and the American Context.* Beirut: Institute for Palestine Studies, 1979.

———. *Peace and Its Discontents:* Essays on Palestine in the Middle East Peace Process. New York: Vintage Books, 1996.

———. *Peace in the Middle East.* Westfield, N.J.: Open Media, 1991.

———. *The Pen and the Sword: Conversations with David Barsamian.* Toronto: Between the Lines, 1994.

———. *The Politics of Dispossession: The Struggle for Palestinian Self-Determination,* 1969–1994. New York: Pantheon, 1994.

———. *A Profile of the Palestinian People.* Chicago, Ill.: Palestine Human Rights Campaign, 1983.

———. *The Question of Palestine.* New York: Times Books, 1979.

———. *Representations of the Intellectual: The 1993 Reith Lectures.* New York: Pantheon, 1994.

———. *The World, the Text, and the Critic.* Cambridge, Mass.: Harvard University Press, 1983.

———, ed. *Kim.* By Rudyard Kipling. London: Penguin Books, 1989.

Said, Edward W. and Fuad Suleiman, eds. *The Arabs Today: Alternatives for Tomorrow.* Columbus, Ohio: Forum Associates, 1973.

Said, Edward W. and Christopher Hitchens, eds. *Blaming the Victims: Spurious Scholarship and the Palestinian Question.* New York: Verso, 1988.

BIBLIOGRAPHY

Interviews

"Interview/Edward W. Said," *Diacritics* 6 (1976): 30–47.

Salusinszky, Imre, "Edward Said," in *Criticism and Society,* by Imre Salusinszky. New York: Methuen, 1987: 123–48.

Wicke, Jennifer and Michael Sprinker, "Interview with Edward W. Said," in *Edward Said: A Critical Reader,* edited by Michael Sprinker. Oxford: Blackwell, 1992: 221–64.

Secondary Sources

Cain, William, "Criticism and Knowledge," review of *The World, the Text, and the Critic,* by Edward Said, *Virginia Quarterly Review* 60 (1984): 181–88. Cain criticizes Said for failing to suggest alternatives to the orthodox, status quo positions in criticism and theory that Said identifies and takes issue with.

———. Review of *Orientalism,* by Edward Said, in *The Crisis in Criticism: Theory, Literature, and Reform in English Studies.* Baltimore: Johns Hopkins University Press, 1984: 209–15. Cain finds contradictions in Said's thesis that all knowledge is fundamentally political.

Gorra, Michael. "Who Paid the Bills at Mansfield Park?," review of *Culture and Imperialism,* by Edward Said, *New York Times Book Review,* 28 February 1993, 11. Gorra praises Said's book but notes that it lacks the originality of his earlier, related study, *Orientalism.*

Kucich, John. "Edward W. Said." In *Dictionary of Literary Biography: Modern American Critics Since 1955,* vol. 67, 249–55. Detroit: Bruccoli Clark/Gale Research, 1988. Kucich provides biographical material on Said and surveys his work through *The World, the Text, and the Critic.*

Leonard, John, "Novel Colonies," review of *Culture and Imperialism,* by Edward Said, *Nation,* 22 March 1993, 383–90. Leonard criticizes Said's book for being disorganized, repetitious, and inaccurate.

BIBLIOGRAPHY

McGowan, John. *Postmodernism and Its Critics.* Ithaca: Cornell University Press, 1991. McGowan is critical of Said's view that though consciousness is always determined by culture, the critic is nonetheless able to step outside and objectively judge his or her culture's values and perspectives.

Morris, Wesley A., review of *Beginnings,* by Edward Said, *Georgia Review* 30 (1976): 736–40. Morris sees Said's book as introducing recent trends in contemporary European theory to an American audience and providing a useful, though incomplete, critique of structuralism.

"Said, Edward W. 1935–." In *Contemporary Authors,* edited by Christine Nasso, vols. 21–24, 759–60. Detroit: Gale Research, 1977.

Sprinker, Michael. "Introduction." In *Edward Said: A Critical Reader,* edited by Michael Sprinker. Oxford: Blackwell, 1992: 1–4. Sprinker provides biographical information on Said and briefly discusses his place and significance in the current critical/theoretical scene.

Young, Robert. *White Mythologies: Writing, History, and the West.* London: Routledge, 1990. Though he is generally complimentary of Said's work, Young criticizes Said for claiming both that consciousness is shaped by culture and that the critic is able to distance him or herself from his or her culture in order to critique it.

Richard Rorty

Primary Works

Rorty, Richard. *Consequences of Pragmatism.* Minneapolis University of Minnesota Press, 1982.

———. *Contingency, Irony, and Solidarity.* Cambridge: Cambridge University Press, 1991.

———. *Philosophical Papers.* Vol. 1, *Objectivity, Relativism, and*

BIBLIOGRAPHY

Truth. Vol. 2, *Essays on Heidegger and Others.* New York: Cambridge University Press, 1991.

———. *Philosophy and the Mirror of Nature.* Princeton: Princeton University Press, 1979.

———, ed. *The Linguistic Turn.* Chicago: Univeristy of Chicago Press, 1970.

Rorty, Richard, J. B. Schneewind, and Quentin Skinnner, eds. *Philosophy in History: Essays on the Historiography of Philosophy.* New York: Cambridge University Press, 1984.

Secondary Sources

Arneson, Richard J., review of *Contingency, Irony, and Solidarity,* by Richard Rorty, *The Philosophical Review* 101 (1992): 475–79. Arenson thinks that Rorty's elevation of the literary critic to the status that philosophers once held is out of date, and he believes that Rorty is too vague in his description of how people should relate to each other in an ideal, liberal society.

Bernstein, Richard J., "Philosophy in the Conversation of Mankind," review of *Philosophy and the Mirror of Nature,* by Richard Rorty, *Review of Metaphysics* 33 (1980): 745–75. Bernstein gives a detailed summation of Rorty's key points and criticizes him for, among other things, claiming that truth is determined entirely by social practices.

Buscemi, William I. "The Ironic Politics of Richard Rorty." *Review of Politics* 55 (1993): 141–57. Buscemi outlines and critiques the major themes of *Contingency, Irony, and Solidarity* and *Objectivity, Relativism, and Truth,* vols. 1 and 2, with an emphasis on Rorty's political thought.

Gowans, Christopher W. "Intuition and Argument in Philosophy: A Critique of Chisholm and Rorty." *International Philosophical Quarterly* 24 (1984): 132–40. Gowans explains and critiques Rorty's rejection, in *Consequences of Pragmatism,* of a certain variety of contemporary analytic philosophy.

Gunn, Giles. *Thinking Across the American Grain: Ideology, Intellect,*

BIBLIOGRAPHY

and the New Pragmatism. Chicago: University of Chicago Press, 1992. Gunn places Rorty in the American pragmatist tradition.

Hacking, Ian, "A Rebirth of Philosophy?," review of *Philosophy and the Mirror of Nature,* by Richard Rorty, *New Republic* 7 October 1981, 33–35. Hacking sees Rorty's book as one that appeals to the average intelligent reader, not solely to professional philosophers.

Norris, Christopher. *Uncritical Theory: Postmodernism, Intellectuals, and the Gulf War.* Amherst, Mass.: University of Massachusetts Press, 1992. Norris criticizes Rorty's neopragmatism, arguing that it provides no way to refute commonly agreed upon ideas with objective facts.

"Rorty, Richard 1941–." In *Contemporary Authors: New Series,* edited by Ann Evory and Linda Metzger, vol. 9, 428. Detroit: Gale Research, 1983.

Shusterman, Richard. "Rorty, Richard." In *The Johns Hopkins Guide to Literary Theory and Criticism,* edited by Michael Groden and Martin Kreiswirth. 626–28. Baltimore: Johns Hopkins University Press, 1994. Shusterman sums up the principal themes of Rorty's major books.

Vann, Richard T., review of *Philosophical Papers,* by Richard Rorty, *American Historical Review* 97 (1992): 799–802. Vann sums up the principal concerns of the two volumes of *Philosophical Papers,* viewing these texts as a useful introduction to Rorty's thought in general.

West, Cornel. *The American Evasion of Philosophy: A Genealogy of Pragmatism.* Madison, Wis.: University of Wisconsin Press, 1989. West places Rorty in the Emersonian tradition of a thinker who values poetry and art more highly than traditional, systematic philosophy.

White, Stephen K., review of *Contingency, Irony, and Solidarity,* by Richard Rorty, *Journal of Politics* 52 (1990): 689–91. White sees Rorty's central concern as the problem of reconciling two principles:

BIBLIOGRAPHY

the right of the individual to construct his or her life in the terms he or she chooses and the need for a society in which people treat each other with kindness and respect.

INDEX

INDEX

INDEX